Nelson Pereira dos Santos

Contemporary Film Directors

Edited by James Naremore

The Contemporary Film Directors series provides concise, well-written introductions to directors from around the world and from every level of the film industry. Its chief aims are to broaden our awareness of important artists, to give serious critical attention to their work, and to illustrate the variety and vitality of contemporary cinema. Contributors to the series include an array of internationally respected critics and academics. Each volume contains an incisive critical commentary, an informative interview with the director, and a detailed filmography.

A list of books in the series appears
at the end of this book.

Nelson Pereira dos Santos |

Darlene J. Sadlier

**UNIVERSITY
OF
ILLINOIS
PRESS**
URBANA
AND
CHICAGO

1 2 3 4 5 C P 5 4 3 2 1

∞ This book is printed on acid-free paper.
Library of Congress Cataloging-in-Publication Data
Sadlier, Darlene J. (Darlene Joy)
Nelson Pereira dos Santos / Darlene J. Sadlier.
p.   cm. — (Contemporary film directors)
Includes bibliographical references and index.
ISBN 0-252-02813-9 (cloth : alk. paper)
ISBN 0-252-07112-3 (pbk. : alk. paper)
1. Santos, Nelson Pereira dos, 1928—Criticism and interpretation.
I. Title. II. Series.
PN1998.3.S26S23   2003
791.43'0233'092—dc21   2002011751

Frontispiece: Nelson Pereira dos Santos (Museum of
Modern Art/Film Stills Archive)

In memory of Helena Salem

Contents |

In the following commentary I have attempted to give a full-scale chronological overview of Nelson Pereira dos Santos's films and a sense of how his work has evolved and been determined by various historical, political, and cultural influences. I provide production information and commentary on each feature film, but have given more attention to some than to others. The reader will find, for example, that I devote considerable analysis to *Vidas secas* (Barren Lives; 1963) and *Como era gostoso o meu francês* (How Tasty Was My Little Frenchman; 1972), which seem to me especially worthy of close viewing and discussion. I would emphasize, however, that dos Santos's work as a whole is rich and complex, and I hope my introduction to his career will prompt further study of films I have not treated in detail.

Until now, no book has been written about Nelson Pereira dos Santos, critical or otherwise, in English. The best comprehensive study in Portuguese is Helena Salem's *Nelson Pereira dos Santos: O sonho possível do cinema brasileiro* (Nelson Pereira dos Santos: The Possible Dream of Brazilian Cinema; 1987), which has been an invaluable source of information. Like all critics of dos Santos, I have also benefited from the seminal works of the North American scholars Randal Johnson and Robert Stam, whose writings are acknowledged at various points in my text.

I wish to thank the Center for Latin American and Caribbean Studies at Indiana University for a travel grant that enabled me to consult film archives and specialists in Rio de Janeiro. In Rio, Silviano Santiago was extremely generous with his time and was instrumental in arranging my interview with dos Santos. Márcia dos Santos provided me with various hard-to-get pamphlets and videos that were essential for writing the book. I received important assistance from staff at the Cinemateca in São Paulo, the Cinemateca at the Museu de Arte Moderna in Rio, and the archives at the Funarte collection in Rio. Carmen Teixeira at the Cinemateca in São Paulo was particularly thoughtful and kind in giving me a personal tour of that impressive facility. Marisa Leal of the Fulbright Commission in Rio has always been extremely helpful whenever I do research in Brazil. I am especially grateful to Nelson Pereira dos Santos, who took time from his busy schedule to engage in an e-mail interview and who graciously responded to many questions that I had while writing the book.

In the United States, Heitor Martins, my colleague at Indiana, read the manuscript and, as always, I benefited from his comments and vast knowledge of Brazil. I am grateful to Gerald O'Grady for granting me permission to republish a long section from his interview with dos Santos from his edited collection *Nelson Pereira dos Santos: Cinema Novo's "Spirit of Light"* (New York and Cambridge, Mass.: Film Society of Lincoln Center and the Harvard Film Archives, 1995). Randal Johnson immediately responded to my e-mail query about the "Manifesto por um cinema popular," and I thank him for sending me a photocopy. The staff at the Museum of Modern Art was very helpful in locating stills for the book. Robert Stam and Martin D'Lugo gave me very helpful suggestions. Finally, I am grateful to Joan Catapano and James Naremore for their support of scholarship on Latin America.

In 1994, I met Helena Salem at a luncheon in Ipanema, and that meeting grew into an all-too-brief friendship that revolved around our interests in movies and literature. In 1995, I invited her to Bloomington, where she gave a lecture on dos Santos's *Memórias do cárcere* (Memoirs of Prison; 1984) for students and faculty in the Department of Spanish and Portuguese. I think Helena enjoyed her short visit to our university town—especially the Chinese dinner with fellow Brazilians (*mineiros*) Heitor Martins and Marlene Martins, who were gracious cohosts and with whom she felt an immediate bond. I admired Helena as a writer and as a person, and her loss is deeply felt. This book is dedicated to her memory.

|||

An earlier version of the material on *Como era gostoso o meu francês* (How Tasty Was My Little Frenchman; 1972) appeared as "The Politics of Adaptation: *How Tasty Was My Little Frenchman*" in *Film Adaptation,* ed. James Naremore (New Brunswick, N.J.: Rutgers University Press, 2000), 190–205.

Nelson Pereira dos Santos

A Cinema of the People |

Nearly fifty years have passed since Nelson Pereira dos Santos made his first film, but he continues to work with youthful enthusiasm on new projects. As this book is going to press he is putting the finishing touches on an ambitious four-part nonfiction series for television about the Brazilian sociologist Gilberto Freyre, author of an internationally renowned study of culture and race in Brazil, *Casa grande e senzala* (The Masters and the Slaves; 1933). Dos Santos credits the French poet Blaise Cendrars, who lived for a while in Brazil and was familiar with Freyre's work, with the idea of making such a film; according to dos Santos, one edition of *Casa grande e senzala* contains a promotional quote from Cendrars, who observed that the book was perfect for adaptation as a motion picture, particularly a documentary (see Barbosa). The adaptation of Freyre's work is also consistent with dos Santos's passion for, if not obsession with, making movies about *o povo* (the people) in the Brazilian Northeast, which is one of the most complex and least understood areas of his country. The form of the television series, which uses a narrative derived from northeastern culture and a diegetic storyteller (the actor and Freyre specialist Edson Nery da Fonseca) conversing with a young student assistant (Vânia Terra), is equally consistent with the strong emphasis on oral culture and narrative frames in dos Santos's later films. When preparing the project, dos Santos was impressed with the eloquence of Freyre's prose, and throughout the initial episode, entitled "O moderno Cabral,"[1] he has Fonseca quote from *Casa grande e senzala* as if it were an epic tale or national legend to be passed down to the next generation. To tell the story, he also follows his typical practice of shooting on location. The film was shot in Recife and Olinda in the northeastern state of Pernambuco, where Freyre was born; at Columbia University, where he studied as an undergraduate; and in Lisbon and Coimbra, where he continued his research on Brazil. The result is perhaps the most wide-ranging and historically rich film of dos Santos's career.

His career is long and quite diverse. Dos Santos began with a groundbreaking neorealist film, which he followed with a series of socially committed works shot mostly on location and generally focusing on the poor and marginal classes; he then experimented with a kind of countercinema that shows the influence of Jean-Luc Godard; and he ultimately returned to a realist form that borrows certain elements from popular entertainment. His various projects are unified by a leftist political point of view and a desire to make his audience think as well as feel. While he has received much critical acclaim and numerous awards—most recently the Gabriel Figueroa Prize from the Los Angeles Latino International Film Festival—he has also had his share of setbacks and disappointments. Particularly remarkable is the sheer number of movies he has made in a country where resources for filmmakers have been in short supply or nonexistent. It took him over two years to raise funds to make the Freyre documentary, whose original format of thirteen episodes had to be reduced to four because of limited resources. But in an interview with Tonico Mercador in April 2000, dos Santos was both sanguine and optimistic about the future of Brazilian cinema:

> For Brazilian cinema to exist there needs to be political support. The people know that a cinema exists, and it only needs a little water to flourish, just a little money to help the films appear. We aren't allowed to have a market of our own. Movie theaters in Brazil are completely dominat-

ed by North American cinema. It's impossible for Brazilian cinema to become self-sufficient in this context. We have a cinema of great vitality, but I believe that filmmaking will continue to be an oppressed activity. When the large mass of Brazilians without shoes, and who are without the resources to enter a movie theater, becomes part of the consumer market, then our cinema will explode and will be preferred by the people because it is ours, because it speaks our language and reflects our innermost beings and reality. That will be like a renaissance.[2] (16)

Given his drive and love of his craft, it is interesting to contemplate what kinds of films dos Santos might have made had he been given a fraction of the multimillion-dollar budgets provided to directors in more industrially advanced countries. But what we tend to prize most about his films—their political awareness, their use of history and literature to comment on and critique the present, their fascination with Brazilian popular culture and religion, their emphasis on race and social class—have less to do with production values than with a perspicacious, humane, and totally uncompromising view of a large, often unstable, culturally rich, and ethnically complex nation. Dos Santos has made movies during good times and difficult times in Brazil; all too often, his films were attacked by government censors, and a few of them, like the now-classic *Como era gostoso o meu francês* (How Tasty Was My Little Frenchman; 1972), were suppressed. Even without allowing for the hardships of making movies under a twenty-year right-wing military dictatorship or the neverending search for financial backers and distributors, his distinguished career has earned him a place among the world's major directors. In looking back over his different stylistic periods and thematic tendencies, we also have the pleasure of looking forward to those films yet to come.

The Apprenticeship Years: São Paulo, Paris, Rio

Nelson Pereira dos Santos, the fourth child in a family of avid moviegoers, was born on October 22, 1928. Despite his mother's desire to name him Marco Antônio, in honor of Anthony, Brazil's patron saint, his father insisted on Nelson after the Lord Admiral Nelson character in Frank Lloyd's 1927 silent film, *The Divine Lady*. In an interview conducted by

Helena Salem, dos Santos credits his parents, and especially his father, for his apprenticeship in the movies: "'My parents were cinephiles. My father in particular was familiar with the whole of silent cinema. He knew everything. . . . But they were spectators and consumers as opposed to trained cinephiles. They were the kind of people who went to the movies to enjoy themselves and to see their idols, the actors. My first contact with the cinema was just that and I was already learning [about movies] by the time I was 10'" (qtd. in Salem 29). Dos Santos's older brother, Saturnino, concurs: "'I think Nelson's love of movies began at those matinee showings.'" He goes on to describe the family's traditional Sunday outing:

"Dad would rent a box at the Cine Teatro Colombo in Brás [São Paulo], a movie theater that had the airs of the Teatro Nacional and was decorated with arabesques, fleur-de-lis, and gold-leaf painting—sensational. Nelson started going when he was just a baby. Mom even took his baby bottle to the cinema. She also brought along water, milk, cheese, bread, salami, and Guaraná [Brazil's national soft drink]. Four hours of movies, from one to five, and this went on for years. We saw all the films considered today to be the great classics of the time as well as all the great actors. The session always began with a documentary, then the comedies followed: Laurel and Hardy, Harold Lloyd, Charlie Chaplin and others." (qtd. in Salem 29)

As this description suggests, the period in Brazilian film history known as the Belle Epoque, which was characterized by a strong national cinema, was long over; by the late 1920s, nearly 85 percent of the movies seen by Brazilians were made in Hollywood. The country's largest movie audiences were located in São Paulo, dos Santos's hometown, which was experiencing a robust, postwar economic period. Movie theaters were renovated to accommodate a growing audience, and new and more luxurious cinemas were built to attract the middle and upper classes. A more sophisticated film literature also began to appear. For example, *Cinearte* offered readers up-to-date information about the Brazilian film industry, with special attention given to the small, regional film companies in Rio Grande do Sul (Porto Alegre), São Paulo (Campinas), Minas Gerais (Belo Horizonte, Pouso Alegre, and Cataguases), and Pernambuco (Recife). Film critics began signing their names to reviews and they became known and trusted for their opinions. A few, such as Guilherme de Almeida, who enjoyed a wide readership for more than fifteen years at *O estado de São Paulo*, were among the most popular figures writing for newspapers (Machado 107–8).

Equally important as the Sunday matinee to dos Santos's apprenticeship was the period he spent as a high school student at the Colégio do Estado Presidente Roosevelt. There he came into contact with a group of young student radicals who raised his awareness of the country's many social and economic problems—especially in nonindustrialized areas like the Northeast. In 1945, dos Santos's commitment to social progress and revolution became so strong that he joined the Partido Comunista Brasilero (PCB) (Brazilian Communist party). The postwar period was an especially heady time for left-wing activists in Brazil. Banned by Getúlio Vargas, the president-turned-dictator, in 1935 following its bloody coup attempt, the PCB was ready to launch a legal comeback under the new Electoral Code. The 1945 elections resulted in major victories for PCB candidates, fourteen of whom were voted into the Chamber of Deputies. After his release under an amnesty law that year, the party's infamous leader, Luís Carlos Prestes, who had been in prison since the 1935 coup, won a seat in the Senate (Page 206).

Dos Santos was a voracious reader while in high school, and it was during this period that he read the novels of Jorge Amado and Graciliano Ramos, two of Brazil's most influential writers, both of whom were from the Northeast. Amado and Ramos wrote compellingly about the rural poor, the urban working class, and the poverty that was endemic to this large area of the country. Both novelists had been persecuted and imprisoned by the Vargas dictatorship in the thirties, and Amado's books were even burned. Dos Santos was drawn to both writers, especially to Amado, and throughout his career he would turn to them for inspiration as well material for the screen.

Dos Santos's commitment to the PCB continued into his university years. Although he decided to pursue a law degree, his left-wing activism and his passion for movies ultimately overshadowed any aspirations he had for practicing law. He spent much of his time editing a literary section of the law school's Communist party publication, *Hoje* (Today), for which he also wrote film reviews. He also participated in political demonstrations on campus and was arrested on more than one occasion.

The popularity of the PCB in cities such as São Paulo was on the rise—so much so that the government of President Eurico Dutra (1945–50) viewed it as a threat. In 1947, Dutra's political supporters took advantage of a clause in the Constitution regarding "antidemocratic" parties, and the Congress banned the PCB from further participation in the political process (Skidmore, *Politics in Brazil* 66). Nonetheless, clandestine meetings and publishing efforts continued to take place in São Paulo and elsewhere, generating anew the atmosphere of political tension and unease of the post-1935 period.

At the same time, São Paulo was undergoing an exciting postwar transformation into one of the modern cultural and industrial giants of Latin America. As the film historian Maria Rita Galvão points out, in the years immediately following World War II, São Paulo became the elected site for some of the country's major cultural institutions, including the Museum of Art, the Museum of Modern Art, the Bienal exposition for the plastic arts, and the Brazilian Comedy Theater (273). Dos Santos took full advantage of these cultural opportunities. In addition to his activities in the PCB, he became a member of theater groups and film clubs; he participated in the first national conferences on cinema in Brazil; and he wrote film reviews for the Communist newspaper *Fundamentos* (Foundations).

The postwar economic boom in São Paulo fed the desire of Brazil's cultural elite for a world-class cinema that would produce technically superior films on the order of Hollywood productions. It was thought that such films would rival and ultimately eclipse the *chanchada* (Brazil's low-budget version of Hollywood musical comedies), a genre that was disdained by most critics but that nevertheless remained extremely popular with the moviegoing public. It is important to note that *chanchadas* were commercially successful at a time when many Brazilian producers and directors found it difficult if not impossible to make movies. *Chanchadas* had tremendous box office draw—especially the Rio-based Atlântida productions, which featured the brilliant comedy team of Oscarito and Grande Otelo. As the director and film historian Alex Viany has remarked: "Oscarito and Grande Otelo were the first great box office names, names that brought people to the movies, names that guaranteed the success of a film. One way or another . . . they put on the screen something with which the people could identify" ("Cinema" 193).[3]

In 1949, the Vera Cruz Film Company was established in São Paulo by some of the same industrialists who had earlier founded the Museum of Modern Art and the Brazilian Comedy Theater. Designed along the lines of the Hollywood studio system, Vera Cruz was a modern and highly ambitious enterprise whose main objective was to produce quality feature films that would attract large audiences and invigorate the nation's film industry. The Brazilian director Alberto Calvalcanti was brought back from Europe, where he had been making films, to head the studio. Between 1950 and 1953, Vera Cruz produced eighteen feature films as well as several documentaries that were technically among the best films ever made in the country—a fact that was credited to the crew of experienced foreign directors and technicians, including the filmmaker Adolfo Celi, the photographer Chick Fowle, and the film editor Oswald Haffenrichter. But as Galvão points out, despite the technical expertise it brought to the productions, Vera Cruz came under attack for its "foreign quality, coming not only from [Vera Cruz's] non-Brazilian directors and technicians, but also from its attempt to imitate 'international standards.'" Galvão adds, however, that in retrospect, "even the most 'foreign' of Vera Cruz's films were more Brazilian than many critics thought at the time. But too often the 'Brazilian-ness' consciously wrought by the filmmakers was limited to exoticism and folklore, while the real problems of the country were ignored" (275). This tendency to exoticize the nation and its inhabitants while neglecting harsh social realities became a source of frequent complaint by reviewers—including the young dos Santos. Ultimately, Vera Cruz produced Lima Barreto's *O cangaceiro* (The Bandit; 1953), a western or "Nordestern" inspired by the legendary bandit Lampião, which became a national and international success. But by that time the company was in severe financial trouble.[4] Just four years after its inception, the first full-fledged attempt at a studio system à la Hollywood went bankrupt and the company closed its doors.

While still a law student, dos Santos decided to go to Paris to study film at the renowned Institut Supérieur d'Études Cinématographiques. Whether because of his timing or because he lacked sufficient funds, he never enrolled in the institute; although he had planned to stay at least a year in Paris, he was forced to return to Brazil after just two months to fulfill his obligatory military service. (He also learned that he was to become a father.) In an interview with Alex Viany, dos Santos reminisces about that short but important period in Paris: "'During that time I did a "film course" at the Cinematheque. [Carlos] Scliar [a Brazilian artist and friend of dos Santos who was studying at the institute] was the "professor": "You have to see this film. You have to see that film." He made a list of required movies. . . . At the time, Vittorio de Sica's *Bicycle Thief* (1948) had just been released. It was an extremely rapid and intensive film education'" (qtd. in Viany, *Processo* 486). After returning to Brazil, he completed his military service and finished law school, although he has never practiced law. In the interview with Viany, he wryly comments that it was only because he assured his law professor that he wanted to make films and had no intention of practicing law or running for a judgeship that he was given a pass on his oral exam and awarded the degree (487).

While finishing his degree, dos Santos made his first film, under a commission from the PCB, a forty-five-minute documentary about young workers in the capital city of São Paulo entitled *Juventude* (Youth). The PCB sent the film to a youth festival in Berlin, but it was never returned and the print was lost. According to dos Santos, the only negative was cut up and pieces of it were used in other PCB documentaries. Despite difficult working conditions and the loss of the print, dos Santos remained positive about his first hands-on experience at moviemaking, stating that it provided him with an important lesson in film editing (Salem 62). A year later, he made a second documentary for the party about the division of labor. "'It was something in which I mixed together anti-Malthusianism, the production of capital and anti-imperialism— all the ideas of the left wing-youth of the period that were so badly digested'" (qtd. in Salem 63).

In 1951, dos Santos worked with Ruy Santos and Alex Viany on an adaptation of *O Saci*, a short story by Monteiro Lobato. Shot in the interior of the state of São Paulo, the film depicts the adventures of Saci Pererê, a one-legged black boy who is a famous character in Brazilian folklore. The film was neither critically nor commercially successful; however, the decision to adapt a work by Monteiro Lobato, a renowned writer who was active in what was to become the left-wing's "Petroleum Is Ours" campaign, brought to the fore the commitment of radical filmmakers to themes and characters representative of the Brazilian working class and its traditions. As a result of his work on *O Saci*, dos Santos was invited by

Ruy Santos to work on another feature, *Aglaia,* which was being filmed in Rio. Dos Santos relocated to Rio, but the film was never completed.

After a year-long interruption in production, the child who played the lead no longer looked like the young character who appeared in the beginning of the film, so the project had to be abandoned (Amancio 14). Nonetheless, dos Santos's temporary move to Rio was both timely and fortuitous. Alex Viany immediately offered him the opportunity to serve as his assistant director on the urban drama *Agulha no palheiro* (Needle in the Haystack; 1953). Bráulio Pedroso, who was associated with *O Saci* and was dos Santos's friend from São Paulo and a fellow member of the PCB, commented on dos Santos's decision to remain in Rio:

"I think Nelson preferred Rio. Perhaps it was also his way of liberating himself from the Mafia of our party's group and from his family. But the rest of us at the time thought that going to Rio was crazy. We thought São Paulo was so much better with Vera Cruz, the TBC [Brazilian Comedy Theater], the Bienal. We looked down on the cinema in Rio, the *chanchadas* of Atlântida. We used to say: poor Nelson. But he had the courage to cut the umbilical cord, and his creativity flourished soon after. While we here [in São Paulo] took years to liberate ourselves." (qtd. in Salem 78)

Toward a Socially Committed Cinema: *Rio, 40 graus*

Once the filming of *Agulha no palheiro* was finished, dos Santos was invited to work on a *chanchada* based on the popular radio program *Balança, mas não cai* (It Swings, but Does Not Fall), which had been adapted for television. Although he was far from enthusiastic about the project, *Balança, mas não cai* was another means to gain experience on a movie set. Like many other films that dos Santos worked on during his career, it, too, was beset by financial problems, and the production came to a halt. By that time, dos Santos had moved his young family to a suburb in Rio close to the studio and at the foot of a what was then the city's largest *favela* (slum). Many crew members lived in the *favela,* and dos Santos came to know the *morro* (hill) and its inhabitants fairly well. It was during this period that the idea for his first feature-length film, *Rio, 40 graus* (Rio, 100 Degrees; 1956), materialized:

I decided to make [the life of the shanty dwellers] into a movie. I wrote a script and tried to make the film, but I wasn't successful. No one liked the idea, and they said: this thing about a *favela* doesn't interest us. . . . But that was Rio, and social problems were very real there because the *favela* is so visible. Evidently they had as many *favelas* in São Paulo as in Rio, but there they were called *cortiços* [tenements]. And because they were spread out horizontally [in São Paulo], they couldn't be seen. You'd drive along the road and you just couldn't see them. But in Rio, the *favela* was highly visible on top of the hill. Now those who live there aren't bothered [by the *favela*]; they've become accustomed to seeing it. But when the *favela* appeared on the screen, they became indignant and said: "That's a lie." (Amancio 16)

According to dos Santos, even the Communist party opposed his idea and its members told him to wait to make the movie until after the revolution, when the people would be in control of the government. But the idea of making a film about shanty dwellers in Rio was in keeping with dos Santos's statements in *Fundamentos* as well as at national cinema conferences, where he spoke about the industry's urgent need to make movies about the real lives, struggles, and hopes of the nation's people.[5] Despite the PCB's strong objections, dos Santos proceeded with his project. His failure to follow the party's directive did have its consequences, however: he was removed from membership on a national committee for cultural affairs and transferred to work with members of a small cell in nearby Lapa and Santa Teresa (Salem 86).[6]

Unable to interest film producers in backing his movie, dos Santos raised funds by establishing a cooperative and selling shares in the film to investors. Even the cast and crew agreed to work for shares. To make the film as inexpensively as possible, expenditures were minimized or avoided altogether. For example, film stock was imported directly from the manufacturer to take advantage of a short-lived Brazilian law that exempted the buyer from paying taxes or customs fees. Humberto Mauro, a major filmmaker in the thirties who became the director of the Instituto Nacional de Cinema Educativo, learned from dos Santos's cameraman, Hélio Silva, that the crew had no equipment to shoot the film, and he agreed to loan them a camera that had to be rebuilt (Salem 86–87).

Rio, 40 graus brings together dos Santos's commitment to the poor and working class and his chief theoretical interests, which, at that time, were shaped by Italian neorealism and Marxism (see Fabris). With the exception of a couple of scenes, the entire movie was shot outdoors using a cast composed primarily of nonprofessionals. It highlights some of Rio's most famous tourist attractions, including Copacabana, Pão de Açúcar (Sugar Loaf), Corcovado, and Maracanã (a huge soccer stadium), but it also shows the city in an entirely new way, mapping its class structure. At the opening is a title card: "Nelson Pereira dos Santos presents the city of São Sebastião do Rio de Janeiro." This is followed by stunning aerial views of Pão de Açúcar, Copacabana, and the chic beach area of the southern zone, or Zona Sul, accompanied by the sound of the popular samba "A voz do morro" (The Voice of the Hill) by the Brazilian composer Zé Kéti. Almost immediately, however, the film establishes a dialectic between postcard views of Rio as the "Marvelous City" and subsequent close-ups of the *favela* in which we see the comings and goings of its inhabitants. In contrast to the aerial shots of the tourist sites, the camera takes a position low to the ground to photograph the *favela* from the base of the hill to the top. This angle enables dos Santos to give audiences a better sense of the size and steepness of the hill as well as the closeness and poverty of the wooden shacks, which lack even running water. We see a boy walking up the hill with a can of water on his head and several others making their way down narrow paths and onto the paved city streets filled with marketplaces, cafés, and palm trees. These few shots make clear that the *favela* is quite close to the city; but life in the metropole is so much richer that it seems like another planet.

Rio, 40 graus is first and foremost an affirmation of dos Santos's belief that Brazilian movies should depict the whole of society, not just the middle and upper classes. If we look at his writings for *Fundamentos,* we find that his two most serious criticisms against films made by Vera Cruz were, first, that they followed Hollywood's model of featuring only whites in the main roles and, second, that they used academic Portuguese in dialogue scenes. In contrast to Vera Cruz productions, *Rio, 40 graus* brings together the stories of men, women, and children who represent the full range of Brazilian society, including its black and mulatto citizenry; the dialogue, for the most part, is an approximation of the language spoken by *o povo.*

Rio, 40 graus's relatively simple plot centers on the adventures of five black youths who leave the hill on a Sunday morning to earn money by selling peanuts in the city (see fig. 1). Their individual adventures take place in and around the tourist sites featured in the opening, thus bringing them into close proximity with the middle and upper-class citizenry, who tend to treat them in guarded fashion or harshly, often for no reason at all. A good example of this kind of interaction occurs early in the film when Paulo, the youngest of the five boys, follows his tiny pet lizard, Catarina, who has leaped out of his hand and raced onto the grounds of the Quinta da Boa Vista, a beautiful park and zoo that is another well-known tourist attraction. Unable to afford the park's admission, the boy slips under a barrier and runs after Catarina, who has taken refuge in a stork cage and comes close to being eaten by one of the birds. Paulo anxiously calls to her, and, like a faithful pet, she runs back to her owner. At this juncture, the film focuses on Paulo as he marvels at the beauty of the Quinta—a bucolic setting filled with trees, birds, and other animals that stands in sharp contrast to the barrenness and poverty of the *favela*. What makes the scene especially endearing are the close-ups of Paulo's cherubic face, which appears to be illuminated from within. Dos Santos also uses a subjective camera to heighten the boy's sense of wonder. This unusually quiet and highly subjective moment in the film is suddenly interrupted by the arrival of the security guard, who treats the small child like a vagrant and proceeds to remove him from the park. When the boy attempts to explain about Catarina and opens his hand to show the lizard to him, the guard snatches her up and tosses her into a nearby cage filled with snakes. The scene ends with one of the snakes slithering toward the harmless and unsuspecting lizard—an image that is mirrored by the predatory-like actions of the guard, who roughly removes Paulo from the park.

The stories of the five peanut vendors are intercut with episodes involving other characters, including a segment dealing with soccer players, club directors, and fans. For the most part, crosscutting or parallel editing between stories is managed in a subtle manner, showing the disparities between the haves and the have-nots. At one point, however, two stories collide in especially dramatic fashion. Threatened by a gang of boys who try to rob him, Jorge runs after a passing streetcar in the hopes of eluding his pursuers only to be run over by an oncoming vehicle. Just at the moment of impact, the film abruptly cuts to the excited faces and cheers of fans at Maracanã stadium, where a nervous replacement player

Figure 1. Peanut vendors in *Rio, 40 graus*. (Nelson Pereira dos Santos collection)

has just scored a goal. By juxtaposing the two scenes this way, dos Santos not only emphasizes the tragedy of the young boy's death, which seems all the more horrific as the soccer fans wave their hands and cheer, but also suggests how the suffering and death of people such as Jorge seem to have little if no impact on the society as a whole.

In other sections of the film, dos Santos tends to be a bit heavy-handed in his depiction of the bourgeoisie and of affluent individuals such as Durão, a major landowner from Minas Gerais who has been elected to the Senate. Accompanied to Rio by his *jagunço* (paid bodyguard), he is loathe to discuss politics and prefers chasing women. The middle-aged and slightly fey Eduardo likes to gossip with young women about the physical attributes of Bebeto, an attractive beach bum and flirt who is interested in the dowry of his recent conquest, Maria Helena (Ana Beatriz). This group of unlikable characters includes Francisco, the father of Maria Helena, who offers up his daughter to the landowner-senator to extract political favors. Meanwhile, American tourists become targets of dos Santos's social critique. Two American women are sitting on a hotel terrace near the sea when one turns to the other and says: "Wonderful country, isn't it?" The other replies, "Yes, but so primitive."

Dos Santos is nevertheless effective in setting up contrasts that point to the economic disparity between the peanut vendors and those with whom they come into contact. In the scene on the beach, Bebeto kicks Jorge's can filled with packets of peanuts into the water. Jorge confronts

A Cinema of the People | 13

him and demands to be reimbursed for his loss. The older and stronger Bebeto pushes the young boy while a well-dressed passerby, who looks at Jorge as if he were the aggressor, stops and says disapprovingly, "These parents who let their children loose in the streets are criminals." The "criminal" in this case is Jorge's ailing mother, Dona Elvira (Arinda Serafim), and the next scene focuses on her desperate situation and her gracious acceptance of help from her neighbor, Ana, who has brought her a plate of food. As in other scenes, the focus here is on the solidarity of the *favelados*. When Dona Elvira expresses concern that Ana has taken over the clothes washing of her clients until she can get back on her feet, Ana replies: "For those who are used to it, there is never too much work. And besides, Dona Elvira, one hand washes the other. The day may come when I'll turn to you for help."

Like many neorealist films made throughout the world in the late forties and fifties, *Rio, 40 graus* is in part a sentimental or even melodramatic allegory about the class system. It tends to portray the middle and upper classes as selfish, judgmental, insensitive, or amoral and the poorer people as fundamentally good and compassionate. For example, the street-wise tough guy Waldomiro (Jece Valadão) takes money from the peanut vendors and repeatedly threatens his former girlfriend, Alice (Cláudia Moreno), who is engaged to another man. The dramatic tension supplied by his character throughout the film reaches a peak at the end, when Waldomiro comes face-to-face with Alice and her fiancé, Alberto (Antônio Novaes). However, just at the point of highest tension, Waldomiro grins and shakes Alberto's hand. His surprising change in demeanor comes about only after he realizes the man is his former comrade in a strike against a local textile mill. The message here and elsewhere in the film, as voiced by Alberto at an earlier point in the movie, is the importance of solidarity among the people as a way to secure a better life for all in the *favela*.

Quite properly, a good deal has been written about the similarity between dos Santos's film and such neorealist classics as Roberto Rossellini's *Rome, Open City* (1945) and De Sica's *Shoeshine* (1946) (see Fabris 91–147). But the specific ideology of *Rio, 40 graus*, as well as the tendency to shade over into a somewhat melodramatic and rhetorical form of cinema, can best be understood if we compare it with a different kind of film, Luis Buñuel's *Los olvidados* (The Young and the

Damned; 1950), which centers on a group of impoverished youths growing up on the streets of Mexico City. In both cases the filmmakers were left-wing artists interested in making a movie that would call attention to the poorest segments of society and specifically to poor children, who were the most vulnerable and presumably innocent victims of the system. And yet, despite the many similarities between the two films, there are significant differences that help to bring dos Santos's approach into clearer focus. Buñuel is merciless in his representation of the bleakness of the children's lives and totally pessimistic about their chances for survival. Dos Santos, on the other hand, is basically optimistic. None of the boys in *Rio, 40 graus* (including the gang members who taunt Jorge) compares with Buñuel's Jaibo, an older delinquent who leads the group and who stalks and kills the young Pedro. No vicious acts are committed by dos Santos's peanut vendors; on the contrary, the emphasis throughout is on their comradeship and solidarity. The treatment of family life is another striking difference. Dos Santos plays up the importance of the home and the goodness of the *favelados* as a counterbalance to their struggle against poverty. The ailing Dona Elvira is kind to her son, Jorge, and he in turn tries to earn money to buy her medicine. When his supply of peanuts is destroyed by Bebeto, he begs for handouts and even steals. Dona Elvira also serves as a mother figure to others. When a policeman brings the orphan Jerônimo back to the *favela*, Dona Elvira claims him as her own even though we know she has little means to support him. The policeman releases the boy to her care—one of the only times in the film that an individual outside the *favela* who is in a position of authority shows any kindness or understanding.

In *Los olvidados,* Buñuel gives another and perhaps less sentimental view of family life. Equally victimized by her economic circumstances, the mother in his film is harsh with her son, Pedro, and ultimately throws him out of the house. At the same time, she becomes infatuated with the delinquent Jaibo, and an Oedipal struggle ensues between the two youths, which is played out in a wrenching dream sequence. This is the only truly surrealistic moment in Buñuel's otherwise (and uncharacteristically) realist film. Pedro dreams that his mother is approaching his bed with a piece of raw meat in her hands; but before he can take the meat, a hand reaches up from under his bed and snatches the piece away. The hand belongs to Jaibo. The final scene in *Los olvidados* shows

Pedro's body being transported to a dump, where it is tossed down a hill. By contrast, *Rio, 40 graus* draws to a close with a party celebrating the crowning of a samba school queen and a return to the aerial shots of Rio. Despite their similarities as radical films made in the fifties, *Los olvidados* is far darker than *Rio, 40 graus,* involves Freud as much as Marx, and offers little hope for the children of poverty. *Rio, 40 graus* is the product of a more straightforward and utopian social realism—the work of a communist filmmaker whose focus is on the economic disparities between the social classes, the integrity and community of the *favelados,* and the possibility of social change and a better life.

Filming of *Rio, 40 graus* began in March 1954, but there were numerous delays because of bad weather and insufficient film stock. A year later, the movie was finished and was approved by the censors for everyone except children ten years of age or younger. Dos Santos signed a deal with the Brazilian branch of Columbia Pictures for the film's distribution and everything appeared to be set for its nationwide release. Just one month after the censors approved the film, however, the head of the Federal Department for Public Safety, Colonel Geraldo de Menezes Cortes, banned it. As Robert Stam points out, Cortes's decision to ban the film most likely resulted from dos Santos's empathetic treatment of black Brazilian youths (161), but publicly Cortes announced that his decision was based upon information that the film was the work of communists who had received financial backing from the Soviet Union. He was also indignant because the film did not portray Brazilians at work. Dos Santos explained that all the events in the film took place on a Sunday, and that even so the peanut vendors and soccer players were shown working; he was also open to a suggestion that a title card be introduced at the beginning of the movie to inform the audience that the action takes place on a Sunday. But the colonel refused to release the film and even held a press conference in which he condemned it as the work of communists who had given a negative view of the city. He declared, among other things, that the title of the film was a lie and that it never got warmer than 30 degrees centigrade in Rio, that the characterization of the senator was an affront to those who served in the Senate, and that the dialogue was offensive because it was filled with grammatical errors and slang.

Cortes's public objections were challenged and deflated by Pompeu de Sousa, editor of the *Diário carioca* (Carioca Daily), and a struggle for the film's liberation ensued. Although there was no law banning private showings, Cortes blocked an attempt to show the film to nearly one thousand people who were waiting in the lobby of the Brazilian Press Association. Following this unprecedented action, letters of protest were sent to President Café Filho as well as to Minister of Justice Prado Kelly. Among the more outspoken critics of the ban was Jorge Amado, who wrote a long editorial for the *Imprensa popular* (Popular Press) in which he attacked the government for its attempts to transform the country into a prison: "'They begin with the film of Nelson Pereira dos Santos and move on to attack theater, literature, painting and music. We're not far from the days of [Vargas's] Estado Novo (New State [1937–45]), when books were unable to circulate and when artists could not paint the figure of a black man'" (qtd. in Salem 118).

Amado's intervention in the debate was important and understandable. A loyal member of the Communist party who was elected to the Congress in 1945, he was sympathetic to dos Santos's project and outraged by the invidiousness of the censors. The decision to ban a film about the plight of the poor at the hands of the wealthy harked back to his own experiences with the censors, who condemned his books for being leftwing and a threat to the nation's welfare. But another aspect of the situation made his protest even more laudable. Amado was one of the first novelists to portray an African Brazilian as a protagonist and hero in Brazilian literature. Among his best works are *Jubiabá* (1935) and *Capitães da areia* (Captains of the Sand; 1937)—both of which portray the adventures of young mulatto and black boys who live in poverty and struggle to survive. In *Jubiabá,* the emphasis is on the need to build political consciousness among the people to address class inequities. The hero of the novel, Antônio Balduíno, not only assumes a political awareness but also becomes more important to the future of the community than the powerful religious leader Jubiabá, who bows to Balduíno in recognition of his significance. *Capitães da areia* focuses on the solidarity of a group of young boys and makes clear the importance of the common political struggle among the poor to overcome social injustice and hardship. One would probably be safe in saying that *Rio, 40 graus* was inspired not only by dos Santos's commitment to people from the *favela* and his admiration for Italian neorealism but also by his reading of Amado, whose works he would later adapt for the screen.

Amado's powerful and eloquent denunciation was followed by a letter with over three hundred signatures, including those of thirty-five Brazilian senators, which was sent to the capital. At the same time, private showings of the movie were held with greater frequency. The film became a cause célèbre—so much so that one newspaper printed the tongue-in-cheek headline: "Cortes Is Principal Publicist for *Rio, 40 graus*" (Salem 119). Dos Santos even received support from a group of French artists and intellectuals, including Yves Montand, George Sadoul, and Simone Signoret, who had learned of the ban and had written a telegram to call for the film's release. What ultimately broke the ban was a failed coup attempt by the right wing to prevent President-elect Juscelino Kubitschek from taking office. With the installation of the new administration, Cortes was forced to leave office; the film was released in December 1955 and was exhibited nationwide the following year.

When *Rio, 40 graus* finally arrived in cities and towns across the nation, huge lines formed at the box offices. Brazilians were excited to see this publicly denounced film. But the public's rush to see the film was short-lived. Dos Santos explains: "'People thought the film had been banned because it contained naked women and other incredible things. They were disappointed when they left the theater, saying that the film was bad—merely a documentary'" (qtd. in Salem 122). Despite the disappointing public reception, *Rio, 40 graus* nevertheless had a startling impact on Brazilian political and cultural life that surely surpassed any expectation the young filmmaker may have had. He also received the first acknowledgment of his international importance as a filmmaker. In 1956, he received the award for best young director at a film festival in Czechoslovakia, and his film was reviewed enthusiastically by the French critic Louis Marcorelles in *Le monde*. In Brazil, critics were nearly unanimous in their praise for the movie. As Glauber Rocha observed many years later in his book *Revolução do Cinema Novo* (1981) *Rio, 40 graus* might be regarded as the developing world's first revolutionary film, since it exploded onto the scene even before the Cuban Revolution (394). Although the critical attention and praise given to the film were important to dos Santos, even more important was his ability to capitalize on his success to make a second feature, *Rio, Zona Norte* (Rio, Northern Zone; 1957) and to produce a third film, Robert Santos's *O grande momento* (The Great Moment; 1958).

Rio, Zona Norte, Mandacaru Vermelho, Boca de Ouro, and the Beginning of the Cinema Novo Movement

The samba music prominently featured in *Rio, 40 Graus* is the focus of dos Santos's second film, *Rio, Zona Norte*, which also takes place in the *favela*. Unlike the first feature, which portrays multiple characters of different ages, races, and social classes, *Rio, Zona Norte* is the story of a single individual, Espírito da Luz Soares (Grande Otelo), a composer of sambas whose poverty forces him to sell his music to those who have the financial means to record it. As Randal Johnson notes, "Like some of dos Santos's later films, notably *O amuleto de Ogum, Rio, Zona Norte* concerns popular culture and its expropriation by the (capitalist) culture industry, notably the mass media (radio) and the largely foreign-owned record industry" (*Cinema* 169). The film is more tightly structured than *Rio, 40 graus;* with the exception of the initial and final scenes, the entire movie is told in flashback by Espírito, who has fallen from a train and is found injured alongside the tracks at the Central Station. Delirious, he begins to recall people and events from his past, including the radio announcer who stole his music; his son who left school, turned thief, and was murdered by a gang; and the woman who left him. He also fantasizes about meeting the singer Ângela Maria, who promised to record one of his sambas.[7]

Filmed on location as well as in the Flama studio, *Rio, Zona Norte* was completed in a record three months and released in November 1957. Expectations for the film were high because of the acclamation for *Rio, 40 graus*. Moreover, the film featured the great cabaret performer and *chanchada* star Grande Otelo (see fig. 2) together with Ângela Maria, who was a popular singer known as "Queen of the Radio." But the reviews as well as the box office returns were disappointing. Among the criticisms lodged against the film was that, despite its title, it had nothing to do with the Rio suburb known as the Zona Norte and that, unlike *Rio, 40 graus*, which brought together life in the city and on the "hill," it focused exclusively on the *favela*. Perhaps unjustly, the film was also characterized as a failed neorealist project. Paulo Emílio Salles Gomes in his article "Rascunhos e exercícios" (Scribbles and Exercises), which appeared in the June 21, 1958, issue of the *Suplemento literário de São Paulo*, was especially vehement in this regard:

Influenced by a film school that sought to escape the studios and seek inspiration in the places, people and situations of an immediate reality, Nelson Pereira dos Santos was perhaps a victim of the illusion that this [neorealist] style exempts him from the toilsome necessity of stylization and the careful acquisition of conventions more adequate for his purposes. He simply places scenes showing a little-worked reality, which are in extremely rough form, into a certain order in the hopes that the poetry and beauty contained in them are communicated spontaneously to the viewer through the miraculous appeal of photography and sound. In reality, the demands of so-called neorealism are more pressing than those of other film schools. . . . The greatest difficulty for the filmmaker whose purpose is to give the impression of an absolute and objective reality is, on the one hand, the need to use all the tricks inherent in the creation of art, and on the other hand, to be obliged to rigorously maintain invisible those resources which he uses in order to achieve this illusion of transparency, of complete adherence to reality, which is characteristic of the genre. (351)

Dos Santos addressed this particular criticism much later in a 1975 publication entitled "Manifesto por um cinema popular," which is regularly attributed to him: "During that period, criticism was neorealist-oriented, but the film wasn't neorealist. The criticism demanded that the film show landscapes of the neighborhoods in the Zona Norte, when that had nothing to do with it. It is a much more psychological film, [nearly] all of which runs through the mind of the composer. He is the one telling his own story" (9). Apparently the director was attempting to make a distinction between the relatively neorealist surface of his film, which involves quasi-documentary, in-the-street photography, and its narrative structure, which is subjective and "psychological." (Here again it should be noted that the psychology is different from what we find in Buñuel's films.) But in an interview given to the *Diário de notícias* (Daily News) four years after the release of *Rio, Zona Norte,* dos Santos acknowledged that films made by himself and others at the time had definite artistic problems and that they were also less than popular with the public. He placed the blame chiefly on the economic situation, which had caused him to wait two years between projects. (*Rio, 40 graus* was shot in 1953–54) and made it difficult to perfect his art:

"We wanted to confront Brazilian reality with our own eyes, with our own way of seeing the world, as if it were original. But there is a considerable distance between that idea and the making of a movie. . . . We want films that communicate. Every filmmaker in the world wants that and one other thing: originality in the way of seeing the world. But few achieve both of these things together. . . . In Brazil, a director makes a film and has to wait years until another opportunity arises. This is detrimental for our cinema. The best time to begin a film is immediately after making one [which allows for an immediate self-critique and] a correcting of the most evident or even the most subtle defects. But that does not happen in Brazil." (qtd. in Fabris 201)

Figure 2. Grande Otelo as Espírito da Luz Soares in *Rio, Zona Norte*. (Nelson Pereira dos Santos collection)

The box office failure of both *Rio, Zona Norte* and *O grande momento*, a movie about an immigrant family in São Paulo produced by dos Santos and directed by Roberto Santos, left dos Santos heavily in debt. He turned to journalism to make a living and pay off his bills, working first at the *Diário carioca* and later at the *Jornal do Brasil*. Although he did not make a feature film for another three years, he managed to keep an active hand in the business by hiring out as a documentary filmmaker. It was while on a documentary assignment in the Northeast in 1958 that he decided to make an adaptation of *Vidas secas* (Barren Lives; 1938), Graciliano Ramos's classic novel about a family of Northeasterners who are forced to migrate across the desert-like *sertão* to survive a drought. Various problems on the set forced him to place that project on hold in 1960. Instead, he filmed *Mandacaru Vermelho* (Red Cactus; 1961), a generic "Nordestern" whose script he wrote and in which he plays the romantic lead.

Anyone who has ever seen *Mandacaru Vermelho* can hardly forget the opening scene, which features a woman with a gun standing on a rock and firing away at unseen targets below her. There is a surrealistic or perhaps campy quality to the image; in fact, the woman's manic behavior here and elsewhere is reminiscent of Mercedes McCambridge's over-the-top performance in *Johnny Guitar* (1954). The plot, moreover, is a fairly conventional love-on-the-run story. Pledged to another, a young girl (Sônia Pereira) falls in love with a ranch hand (dos Santos) who works for her aunt (Jurema Penna) (see fig. 3). When the girl discovers that her aunt is responsible for the death of her parents (the killing scene that begins the film), she decides to run away with the ranch hand, whose brother, a strangely stalwart yet unsympathetic figure, helps them cross the *sertão* to reach a priest who will marry them. Their plan is discovered, and the aunt, her brother, and her two sons chase the trio across the backlands to the place known as Mandacaru Vermelho, which is also where the girl's parents were ambushed and gunned down. A religious recluse now resides there, and in one of the film's most bizarre scenes he performs a "ceremony" to unite the couple while bullets fly around their heads. The couple are the only ones to survive the shoot-out, and they press on, reaching a small town just in time to be married by a priest who is performing an outdoor marriage ceremony for the town's young couples.

Figure 3. Nelson Pereira dos Santos as the ranch hand and Sônia Pereira as the niece in *Mandacaru Vermelho*. (Cinemateca Brasileira, São Paulo)

Filming of *Mandacaru Vermelho* took place over a two-month period and the movie was released in 1961. In an interview given shortly before the film's opening, dos Santos sounds almost self-effacing, perhaps realizing in advance how the film would be received: "'*Mandacaru* is a totally new and unexpected experience for me. Had it not been for a flood that interrupted and shut down the production [of *Vidas secas*], I believe it would have been difficult for me to make a film like *Mandacaru Vermelho*. This isn't meant as an understatement or a preview of a forthcoming apology. I simply mean that in the whole of my work there isn't any film that looked to fantasy . . . without being preoccupied with an analysis of society'" (qtd. in Salem 150). Although *Mandacaru Vermelho* failed miserably at the box office, it did receive some favorable press—most prominently in a review written by Cláudio Mello e Souza for the *Jornal do Brasil*. One important point he makes is that the film totally avoids the exoticism generally associated with the Northeast. "'On the contrary,'" he writes, "'it's a film that exposes the Brazilian Northeast and certifies its tragic, primitive, and at times grotesque reality, giving it a dramatic, even if precarious, dimension'" (qtd. in Salem 151). Johnson has observed more recently that the film not only anticipates Glauber Rocha's *Deus e o Diabo na terra do sol* (Black God, White Devil; 1963) but also functions as a preview of the "violent universe of the *sertão*" that would become a trademark of the Cinema Novo (*Cinema* 172).

In fact, it was during the filming of *Mandacaru Vermelho* that dos Santos came to know Glauber Rocha, a young Bahian filmmaker who worked with him on the movie. Their friendship and collaboration continued when they returned to Rio, where Rocha had plans to edit his first feature film, *Barravento* (The Turning Wind; 1961), about a fishing village's struggle with commercial exploitation and religious alienation. Working for meager wages, dos Santos supervised the editing of *Barravento*. According to Rocha, it was from dos Santos that he learned how to use and control cinematic language (Viany, "Cinema" 188). Dos Santos also shared his editing expertise with other young directors. For example, that same year he helped the newcomer Sérgio Ricardo on *O menino de calça branca* (The Boy in White Pants); the following year, he edited Leon Hirszman's *Pedreira de São Diogo* (São Diogo Quarry). The latter was a segment in the feature-length film *Cinco vezes favela* (Slum Times Five), a collaborative effort produced by the Centro de Cultura Popular, which brought together the filmmakers Marcos Farias, Miguel Borges, Carlos Diegues, and Joaquim Pedro de Andrade. Shortly thereafter, Hirszman, Diegues, and Andrade, along with dos Santos and Rocha, would become among the country's best-known directors as well as the central figures in the Cinema Novo movement.

As Rocha points out in *Revisão crítica do cinema brasileiro* (Critical Review of Brazilian Cinema; 1963), 1962 was a banner year for the Brazilian movie industry. Among the productions either completed or in the works were Roberto Pires's *A grande feira* (The Great Marketplace) and *Tocaia no asfalto* (Ambush on the Highway), Ruy Guerra's *Os cafajestes* (The Scoundrels), the Centro de Cultura Popular's *Cinco vezes favela*, Anselmo Duarte's *O pagador de promessas* (Journey to Bahia), Paulo Saraceni's *Porto das caixas* (Port of Boxes), Alex Viany's *Sol sobre a lama* (Sun over the Mud), and dos Santos's *Boca de Ouro* (Gold Mouth) and *Vidas secas* (50). According to newspaper reports at the time, Pires's *A grande feira*, about a protest against an official attempt to ban a popular marketplace to appease local businessmen, was as successful at the Brazilian box office as Hollywood's remake with Charlton Heston of the epic *Ben-Hur* (Fernão Ramos 332). *O pagador de promessas*, about a poor farmer's pledge to carry a large wooden cross to Salvador if the Virgin Mary would cure his ailing burro, won the Palme d'Or at the Cannes Film Festival. *Os cafajestes*, which exposes male middle-class depravity at the expense of unsuspecting young women, surpassed all previous box office receipts for a Brazilian movie—most likely because of the censors' furor over the film's lurid portrait of the bourgeoisie and the nude scenes featuring the popular actress Norma Bengell.

Dos Santos's fourth film, *Boca de Ouro*, was among the commercial successes that year. The film was an unusual project for a left-wing director because it was based on a work by the well-known ultraconservative playwright Nelson Rodrigues. Dos Santos says that he encountered considerable pressure and opposition when word got out that he was about to make the film because Rodrigues was considered taboo by the Left (Amancio 26). But dos Santos had been approached by Jece Valadão (Rodrigues's brother-in-law), who had worked on *Rio, 40 graus* as both actor and assistant director and who was eager to follow up his recent acting success as one of the "scoundrels" in Guerra's *Os cafajestes*. Perhaps dos Santos agreed to do the project, which was produced by a collective, simply to continue directing films, but it is just as likely that he was eager to try his hand at adapting a successful work of literature to the screen. (The play had had a successful run at the Teatro Nacional de Comédia in Rio and a touring company took it throughout Brazil.) Despite Rodrigues's politics, dos Santos regarded the play as a fascinating psychological study of a marginal segment of society located in Rio's suburban Zona Norte (see Xavier, "Golden").

The title character (Jece Valadão) is a racketeer who robs and kills at will and gets away with his crimes by bribing public officials. His unusual name derives from his decision to have all of his teeth removed so that he can wear a set of dentures made of gold. He is obsessed with wealth and fame, and he proudly proclaims that when he dies, he will be carried off to his grave in a gold coffin. Constructed along the lines of Akira Kurosawa's *Rashomon* (1950), the plot centers on three different versions of a story, all of which are told by Boca's ex-girlfriend, Guigui (Odete Lara), to a newspaper reporter (Ivan Cândido) sent to her house to get a feature on the recently murdered mobster. Now a housewife with two children, Guigui, who is unaware of Boca's death, tells the reporter that Boca is a dog and a killer, and she proceeds to recount one of his more heinous crimes. The film turns to the past as Guigui begins her story.

In exchange for a loan from Boca, a young husband, Leleco (Daniel Filho), agrees to send for his wife, Celeste (Maria Lúcia Monteiro), whom Boca has designs on and insists must ask him for the money. When Celeste arrives and refuses Boca's sexual advances, he calls to the husband, who is seated in an adjacent room; Boca tells the husband that unless his wife complies with his wishes, he will be killed, and he pulls out a gun to back up his threat. Shaking and crying, Leleco tells his wife to go into Boca's bedroom. Despite the husband's onerous complicity, Boca hits him on the head with the pistol and then beats him to death on the floor.

In telling the story, Guigui is pleased that Boca's crime will be exposed in the newspaper; that is, until she learns by chance that Boca has been murdered. Shocked by the news, she cries hysterically and then runs after the reporter, who has left to file his story. Catching up to him in the street, she recants her initial statement and proceeds to tell another version of the incident, which we then see on the screen. This time Boca is portrayed as a benevolent patron whom Celeste has sought out for money (see fig. 4). She is as dazzled by his money as he is by her breasts, which she exposes to him to get a diamond necklace. Having followed Celeste to Boca's house, Leleco pulls a gun and threatens him. In an attempt to protect Boca, whose wealth she prefers over the poverty of her husband, Celeste plunges a knife into Leleco's back.

Following this story, Guigui tells the reporter still another version to assuage the hurt feelings of her husband (Adriano Lisboa), who is jealous of Guigui's more than tender feelings for Boca. In this account, Leleco learns that Celeste is having an affair with Boca. Celeste goes to Boca and warns him that her husband now knows of their relationship. Leleco arrives and tries to extort money from Boca, who pulls a gun and incites Celeste, who stabs her husband in the back. Boca finishes the job by beating Leleco with his gun. Later on, Boca slits Celeste's throat and then makes sexual advances to the more sophisticated and well-to-do Maria Luíza (Geórgia Quental). At the end of the film we discover that Maria Luíza is the one responsible for Boca's murder.

Figure 4. Jece Valadão as Boca de Ouro and Maria Lúcia Monteiro as Celeste in *Boca de Ouro*. (Museum of Modern Art/Film Stills Archive)

Like many of Rodrigues's plays, *Boca de Ouro* focuses on the depravity of individuals who appear unable or unwilling to change. The film, like the play, lays bare the sordidness of characters's motivations and the deviousness of their actions. Guigui's different versions of Boca's exploits enable the film to become a psychological tour de force emphasizing sex, greed, and jealousy. Ultimately, we can never know which of the three stories about Boca is true, just as we can never be sure which of the three Guiguis (irate, tender, contrite) shows her true character. The idea of fakery or falsehood is everywhere in the film. Even Boca's name no longer rings true when it is discovered that he lies toothless in his coffin, which is nothing more than a cheap pine box.

Although the film is faithful to the sensationalism of the original play—to the point that it includes a particularly scandalous scene of Celeste and three upper-middle-class socialites baring their breasts to Boca in a competition for a diamond necklace—Rodrigues felt that dos Santos had "puritanized" the story. Dos Santos claims that he did not change a word of Rodrigues's text, but he decided not to hire actors who had been part of the play's success; instead, he contracted actors who had no theatrical experience, such as Odete Lara, who was a popular movie star and sex symbol and whose performance as the chameleon-esque Guigui is one of the highlights of the film. Although dos Santos filmed most of the movie in a studio, he also shot several scenes outdoors, partly to "open out" the play but mostly to give audiences a better feel for the Zona Norte. The film begins with a few outdoor shots composed in a masterful montage that shows Boca at various moments in his career as a gambler, a ruthless killer, and a political power in the city. This action-filled prologue, over which the credits are displayed, runs for several minutes without a single line of dialogue. The images of gangsters, police, robbery, and shoot-outs played off against a jazz score give the film the look and sound of a Hollywood film noir, although whether dos Santos means it as a tribute or a parody of low-budget crime pictures is open to speculation.

Although *Boca de Ouro* was popular with film audiences and became dos Santos's first commercial success, the reviews overall were not favorable. The ideological divide between the film critics, who were left-wing and neorealist, and Rodrigues, who was a playwright and conservative aesthete, was simply too wide. Hugo Barcellos's commentary in the *Diário de notícias* exemplifies the kind of criticism the film received: "'Nelson with Nelson doesn't work. And it doesn't work because Nelson Pereira dos Santos, highly faithful (so they say) to the original text by Nelson Rodrigues, allowed himself to be blinded by the artificiality of the playwright'" (qtd. in Salem 157). A less acerbic review was written by Luiz Alberto Sanz, who seems to have been sensitive to the politics behind the film's unfavorable critical reception. Writing for the *Jornal do comércio,* Sanz argues that *Boca de Ouro* was an adult film that "'deserved a calm and careful examination, free of the prejudice that favors the nascent Cinema Novo'" (qtd. in Salem 158). In a more recent assessment, the film historian Fernão Ramos also feels that dos Santos needs to be viewed as unique in relation to Cinema Novo: "Despite his identification with 'the young [directors],' [dos Santos] maintains . . . the personal touch of a filmmaker from another generation, even if at times it flows together with the [Cinema Novo] movement as a whole. *Boca de Ouro* is . . . an example of this duality" (348).

As we have seen, Brazilian directors were receiving widespread critical notice in 1962 and their films were shown at festivals in Brazil and abroad, where a few were awarded prizes. The expression *Cinema Novo* was coined in this period by the film critic Ely Azeredo to describe the groundswell of mostly low-budget, socially committed films that began to appear on the screen in the early sixties. Azeredo attributes special importance to *Rio, 40 graus* because of its "bravery at breaking through the limitations of a cinema imprisoned within the studio system . . . and for its shocking, naked view of reality that the Italian cinema had experimented with in *Rome, Open City* (1945) and *Paisan* (1946)" (7). He also credits Viany's *Agulha no palheiro* (which dos Santos helped to direct) as well as Roberto Santos's *O grande momento* (which dos Santos produced) as other important precursors of the movement.

According to Glauber Rocha, the movement's leading theoretician, the phrase *Cinema Novo* emerged in one of the meetings of the Rio-based Associação Brasileira de Cronistas Cinematográficos, which was headed by Azeredo and others. This group wanted to have better contacts with filmmakers and dialogue among filmmakers, and the members even discussed the possibility of a film journal called Cinema Novo (Viany, "Cinema" 186). But the beginnings of the movement date back to 1959–60, when a new generation of film enthusiasts gathered in the cinema clubs and in the Grupo de Estudos Cinematográficos (associated with the Metropolitan Union of Students) and began to write about movies for the *Jornal do Brasil* and *O metropolitano* which was the newspaper of the union. Some of these young men went on to become film critics; others took up filmmaking; and a few, like Rocha, did both. As Azeredo notes, with the fall of Vera Cruz and the transference of the *chanchada* from movie screens to television, the idea of a new and daring cinema began to intrigue some producers. Ruy Guerra's *Os cafajestes* was a low-budget film in the style of the French New Wave; *O pagador de promessas* was a more costly and ambitious enterprise that exemplified the eclecticism of the Cinema Novo movement. "'It isn't by chance that *O pagador de promessas* brought together a Paulista director [Anselmo Duarte], who was a former leading man at Atlântida and Vera Cruz, with a Bahian writer [Dias Gomes] who was experienced in radio-theater, and a Paulista actor [Leonardo Vilar] from the TBC [Brazilian Comedy Theater]'" (Viany, qtd. in Azeredo 10). In an essay on the Cinema Novo, Azeredo lists Cesare Zavattini, Sergei Eisenstein, René Clair, and cinema verité as influences on the young Brazilian directors

(10). According to Rocha, the contact he had with Europe via letters sent to him by his friends Andrade, Gustavo Dahl, and Saraceni, who went to Italy to study film, was vital to his theoretical orientation while his work with dos Santos on editing prepared him for his next feature, *Deus e o Diabo na terra do sol* (Viany, "Cinema" 188).

It is important to emphasize that the Cinema Novo's agenda for a national cinema harks back to the early fifties (if not earlier), when dos Santos, Viany, and others were publicly decrying how dependent the local market was on the indiscriminate importation of foreign films and how dependent most directors were on the reigning influences in Hollywood. As dos Santos points out in a 1965 interview: "'At the time of Vera Cruz, whoever talked about an independent production was committing a heresy. Cinema could only be made on the basis of the studio, the great industry, the great capitals in this industry, on the basis of the great film star, and so on. The mentality of Brazilian cinema was exactly that and it ruined an entire generation'" (qtd. in Viany, "Cinema" 190). In the same interview, Rocha points out that it was not only local independent filmmaking that was marginal but also Brazilian film criticism. A major difference between the early fifties and the early sixties was that many more critics were writing about film in the sixties and they were having an impact on the culture; in other words, film was no longer regarded as marginal or secondary to the other arts. Viany adds in this interview (and his view has become commonplace today) that the *chanchada* contributed significantly to Cinema Novo as the first legitimate attempt in Brazilian cinema to portray different social types and ways of speaking. There was a communication between the *chanchada* filmmakers and the public, he argued (193), and this communication was equally important to Cinema Novo directors, who were eager to raise the consciousness of *o povo* with realist films about poverty and class struggle as well as films that focused on topics such as African-Brazilian religion and Northeastern popular culture. Despite festival triumphs and critical acclaim, however, the films associated with Cinema Novo rarely appealed to mainstream audiences, who continued to prefer glossy Hollywood entertainment over what Rocha describes in his manifesto, "Uma estética da fome" (An Aesthetic of Hunger; 1965), as Cinema Novo's "sad, ugly . . . desperate, screaming films"—Brazil's version of what the critic Benedito J. Duarte referred to in 1947 as the Italian "cine de fome" (cinema of hunger).

Fernão Ramos's commentary on *Boca de Ouro*, which notes the uniqueness of dos Santos's work in relation to the Cinema Novo, raises an important issue. Cinematic schools or movements are usually more heterogeneous than critics realize. They take shape out of a need for collective publicity or national identity, and their aims are often oversimplified. As dos Santos himself explains in a 1999 interview, he was already working on his fifth film when the Cinema Novo movement took hold, and he modestly claims to have been "coopted" by the group:

"The wave of Cinema Novo is on the one side Glauber [Rocha], and Leon [Hirszman] and Joaquim Pedro [de Andrade]. Joaquim Pedro was in the School of Philosophy and Leon was in the School of Engineering. Then there was the student film movement and on the other side, Cacá [Carlos Diegues] and then [Arnaldo] Jabor. Law School, PUC [Pontifícia Universidade Católica], etc. But they all got together. They're people who have quite different backgrounds. . . . Everyone asks me: what is the ideology of Cinema Novo? An ideology of Cinema Novo didn't exist; each one had his own point of view. Some had relations with the left, which in that period was the Communist Party. And others had another political view of the world, more centrist, more connected to the church, which is the case of Cacá. It wasn't a solid entity or a single thought. And no one was obliged to make movies from a social perspective. . . . The idea was to make films, the best ones possible. . . . But as I was saying, I was coopted. Another important point: I was ten years older than they were." (Amancio 34–35)

Vidas secas

Dos Santos's best pictures sometimes offer brilliant translations of literature into another medium, but he is neither an illustrator of classics nor a proponent of what François Truffaut once derided as a "tradition of quality." A committed director, he tends to have left-wing sources for his films and adopts largely proletarian themes. Many of his adaptations can be seen as responses to the turbulent decades when Brazil moved from an unstable left-labor government to a right-wing military rule and finally to a nascent redemocratization. Throughout the sixties and early seventies, dos Santos used canonical literature as an indirect way of speaking about contemporary social problems. He chose safely historical texts, but the texts contained themes that spoke directly to his audiences.

An obvious case in point, and one of the most important films in dos Santos's career, is *Vidas secas,* a sort of Brazilian version of *The Grapes of Wrath* (albeit a much more raw and less sentimental narrative than we find from either John Steinbeck or John Ford). The corrupt landowning system and the brutally impoverished peasantry described in the 1938 novel by Graciliano Ramos were still in place when the film was released; indeed, the labor government headed by João Goulart proposed a partial agrarian reform system that very year, and a middle-class revolt against reforms of this nature, which included the nationalization of privately owned petroleum refineries, led to a new conservative regime in 1964 (Poppino 280). Although dos Santos placed a title at the beginning of *Vidas secas* to inform viewers that the action took place in 1941, most Brazilians and virtually any traveler to the country's Northeastern provinces would have seen that the film was a kind of docudrama about contemporary conditions and a direct intervention in the political debates of the day.

As noted earlier, dos Santos traveled from Rio to Bahia and Pernambuco in 1958 to make a documentary about a drought that had been ravaging the *sertão* since the previous year. At the time, there was widespread discussion about agrarian reform and peasants were challenging the political authority of landowners by claiming the right to remain on properties where they lived and worked, as well as legal title to the land (Tavares 24). Dos Santos was eager to participate in the discussion by means of a film that would present a straightforward, unsentimental portrait of the Northeast. *Vidas secas* was an ideal choice for a project of this type; it was also a major work of Brazilian literature that he looked forward to adapting to the screen (Cárdenas 64–65).

Work on the film was set to start in early 1960 in a small town in Bahia. But instead of finding the dry, hot, and sunny weather that was customary for the summer months, he encountered overcast skies, so shooting had to be delayed. Unexpected rains that flooded the town caused further delays, and the cast and crew began joking that the film would have to be changed from *Vidas secas* (which literally means "Dry

Lives") to *Vidas molhadas,* or "Drenched Lives." At this point, dos Santos decided to make *Mandacaru Vermelho.* A year later, in 1962, he returned to *Vidas secas.* This time he moved the location farther north to Palmeira dos Índios, a town in the state of Alagoas, which was where Graciliano Ramos had served as mayor and had written his first novels. The weather cooperated, as did the locals, several of whom, including Jofre Soares, in his first acting role as the landowner, and the dog, Baleia, appear in the film.

Released in 1963, *Vidas secas* generated considerable critical attention and was especially praised for the photography of Luiz Carlos Barreto, who had largely abandoned the use of camera filters to capture the glare and brilliance of the northeastern sun.[8] Despite early favorable notices, the film received limited distribution in Brazil. The journalist and film critic Ely Azeredo complained that MGM, who had contracts with the Rio cinemas where the film briefly appeared, had purposely kept the run short, fearing its success would somehow open the door to a more competitive Brazilian film industry. Herbert Richers, the executive producer of *Vidas secas,* said merely that while the picture was a critical success, it was not especially popular with the moviegoing public. According to Richers, the film just managed to recover its costs, and that was only because of the cash prize given to it by Carlos Lacerda, the governor of Guanabara, who had seen the movie and was deeply impressed by it (Salem 174–75).

In 1964, a year after its release, *Vidas secas* was selected to compete along with Glauber Rocha's *Deus e o Diabo na terra do sol* at the Cannes Film Festival, where it was considered to be a strong competitor for the Palme d'Or. (The prize ultimately went to Jacques Démy's *The Umbrellas of Cherbourg.*) Five years later, *Vidas secas* finally premiered in the United States and was reviewed in the *New York Times* by Vincent Canby, who was moved by the portrait of a poverty "so complete, so hopeless, that it isn't just a state of being but something as unfathomable (to one who does not know it) as another dimension in time." Canby was especially struck by the focus on "poverty's small subsidiary horrors," and he rightly described the film as a cinematic "call to arms" (30). Over the years, it has become synonymous with the Cinema Novo movement, and to this day it continues to be a forceful account of underdevelopment and vast socioeconomic disparities that plague the Northeast (see fig. 5).

Figure 5. Átila Iório as Fabiano and Maria Ribeiro
as Sinhá Vitória in *Vidas secas*. (Museum of
Modern Art/Film Stills Archive)

Vidas secas was dos Santos's first adaptation of a work by Ramos, who died in 1953. As dos Santos's stated some twenty years after making the film:

> "No other [Brazilian] novelist had such a sense of dramatic value or such admirable and keen psychological insight. The characters that he created were not puppets or contrived creations or simple shadows that appeared out of the novelist's imagination. On the contrary, they were living beings of flesh and bone, blood and nerves and with logical responses and actions that always followed deep-rooted motivations. There are no inconsequential or artificial types in his books. For that very reason they seduce a filmmaker's imagination, on the level of characters created by a Tolstoy or Dostoevski." (qtd. in Salem 173–74)

Dos Santos had written to Ramos in the early fifties to discuss filming an adaptation of his earlier novel, *São Bernardo* (1934), a compelling story about a despotic plantation owner whose violence and jealousy force his wife to commit suicide and ultimately bring about his own demise.

In his letter, dos Santos asked Ramos how he would feel if he changed the plot so that the wife would leave her husband instead of taking her life. Ramos rejected the proposed change, arguing that it would be historically inconsistent with the society and period he was writing about; he also emphasized the importance of maintaining the story structure and what he referred to as the "essence" of the work.[9]

Nearly twenty years after the release of *Vidas secas*, dos Santos's ideas about adaptation seemed to concur with Ramos's response: "'Adaptation is not a prison. . . . [It] leads to great discoveries. . . . The essence of the book and its narrative structure . . . are a great stimulus that leads me to find solutions that neither minimize nor conceal the author's universe'" (qtd. in Salem 171). At the time *Vidas secas* was released, however, dos Santos said little or nothing about his "great discoveries" and "solutions," some of which had led him to depart from the original text and all of which give the film a greater political efficacy. To avoid any problems with the censors, he began *Vidas secas* with a title card emphasizing the film's "faithful transposition" of an "immortal work of Brazilian literature." And yet his adaptation involved several important changes in plot structure, narration, and language.

Ramos's novel about the peasant Fabiano (Átila Iório) and his family had grown out of a published short story, "Baleia" (Whale), about the death of the family's dog; this and a few other stories were used to help make up the thirteen relatively independent sections of the book. Critics have often commented on the novel's modular structure of "nuclear narratives," some of which can be moved around in relation to one another without changing or jeopardizing the overall meaning. Dos Santos takes certain liberties with the ordering of events—most significantly by moving the highly emotional scene of Baleia's death closer to the end of the narrative and just prior to the family's renewed attempt to escape from the drought. Even in the novel, the scene is especially moving because of the family's love for the dog, who early on saves them from starvation by killing a small, rodent-like creature called a cavy. Baleia is Fabiano's constant companion and helpmate, rounding up goats for the boys, who gesture and call out in the tradition of their *vaqueiro* (cowboy) father. Halfway through the novel, Baleia is stricken by what appears to be rabies, and Fabiano decides to put her out of her misery. As Fabiano takes aim with a rifle, Baleia tries to elude him by hiding behind trees and scrub brush. Fabiano's distraught wife, Sinhá Vitória (Maria Ribeiro), presses her two young sons to her sides, struggling to spare them from the inevitable gunshot by covering their two exposed ears with her hands.

By moving this sequence closer to the end of the film, dos Santos heightens its emotional effect. His adaptation also reveals a basic difference between the media of prose and film, since it dramatizes actions that are only described in the novel, using real actors. The scene of the dog's slow demise from a gunshot shows her quietly contemplating a few cavy that she would normally bark at and chase; as the sun sets in the background, we see her eyes slowly closing in death. This shot had a startling impact when the film was shown at the Cannes Film Festival. Baleia's death was so realistic that many were convinced that the dog had actually been shot and killed. The concern about the dog's fate was so overwhelming that a formal protest was launched by the Animal Rights Association of France. One French reviewer referred to the death scene as "abominable." To quell the growing criticisms and protest, dos Santos sent for Baleia, who was flown from Rio to Cannes, where she quickly assumed celebrity status. According to the cinematographer Luiz Carlos Barreto, he and dos Santos were obliged to take the dog with them wherever they went. Shortly after Baleia's arrival in Cannes, they were asked to appear with her at a photo shoot near the entrance to the film festival grounds. Barreto recalls the pandemonium of that day as a result of the legion of photographers who had unexpectedly shown up to take Baleia's picture (Salem 178–79).

As Johnson has pointed out in his important 1981 essay, "*Vidas secas* and the Politics of Filmic Adaptation," dos Santos also took liberty with the frequency of events in the novel by collapsing into a single long segment three chapters that describe three separate visits to a nearby town made by Fabiano alone or with his family. The three chapters are important because they enable us to see the country in relation to the town, and they provide a sort of cognitive mapping of social class and political power. Dos Santos may have decided to combine them for economic reasons or in consideration of the film's running time—especially since he added new material in the form of a *bumba-meu-boi* (a popular celebration performed during the Christmas season) as well as an encounter between Fabiano and a young man who later invites him to join his band of armed mercenaries. Although it seems unclear whether the film's collapsing of the three town scenes into one provides what Johnson views as a greater linearity and coherency to the narrative, the change undoubtedly alters the novel's repeated suggestion that the town holds nothing positive for the *retirante* (peasant migrant).

The three sections, separated from one another in the book, describe Fabiano feeling ill at ease in crowds indoors and on the streets, being swindled by his landowner boss (Jofre Soares) and shopkeepers, and being harassed and ultimately imprisoned for a short time by a local official referred to as "the yellow soldier" (Orlando Macedo). Here it might be noted that in March 1936, Ramos, who was then director of public instruction in Alagoas, was himself imprisoned by the right-wing government of Getúlio Vargas on suspicion of being a Communist. Ramos was never formally charged during his ten-month incarceration, which he wrote about in his posthumously published *Memórias do cárcere* (Memoirs of Prison; 1953) and which dos Santos adapted for the screen in 1984. There is no question that Ramos's harrowing experiences as a prisoner also influenced his writing of *Vidas secas*. In one of the novel's most disturbing scenes, the yellow soldier invites Fabiano to join a card game in which both men lose their money. The yellow soldier takes out his anger at having lost by following and pushing Fabiano, who has left the game and is on his way home. When Fabiano swears at the yellow soldier, who provokes him further by grinding his boot heel into Fabiano's sandal-covered foot, the yellow soldier has him arrested and taken to jail. There Fabiano is unjustly accused of something "heinous"— an accusation that he does not understand and to which he fails to respond. The police whip him mercilessly on the back and chest with the flat of a large knife blade and then push him into a dark jail cell. Lying on the cell floor, Fabiano strives to comprehend the reason for his arrest: "He was ignorant, yes, sir, he had never been taught and he didn't know how to explain himself. Was this why he was imprisoned? How was that? A man can be put in jail because he doesn't know how to speak well? What harm did his ignorance cause?" (Graciliano Ramos 48).

The town also invokes fear in Sinhá Vitória and her sons, who accompany Fabiano to town to attend a church service. In the section of the novel ironically entitled "Celebration," Sinhá Vitória leaves the church with her sons and suddenly experiences an urgent need to urinate.

Unfamiliar with the town, she has no idea where to relieve herself. Embarrassed and humiliated, she finally lifts her skirts and urinates in the street while trying to avoid ruining her only good pair of shoes. An equally perplexed and worried feeling comes over the two young boys. Accustomed to their solitary life in the countryside, they are amazed by the crowds and the various unknown commodities offered on the streets and in shop windows; they are especially frightened when their companion and frequent source of comfort, Baleia, suddenly disappears.

While the book emphasizes the various difficulties that the *retirante* confronts during even the briefest trips to town (a pattern that has obvious significance when the family decides at the end of the novel to migrate to the city), the film, which dispenses with chapter titles, provides a realist portrait of an area of the country that is often viewed from the outside as "quaint." The *bumba-meu-boi* is a good example of a popular cultural phenomenon that has been transformed into an entertainment commodity in provincial towns and big cities. Audiences pay to see the celebration performed on stage and, knowingly or not, sit in for the landowning class for whom the workers toil. The audience watches them "perform" their daily lives and symbolically slay an ox. Dos Santos places the *bumba-meu-boi* in a context that reaffirms its popular yet feudal character. Among the group of workers in ceremonial dress is a harlequin in blackface who, reminiscent of a court jester, sings comic verses to entertain the landowner and other town leaders. Although the ceremony is performed by workers in the street, we can also see the village gentry sitting on a veranda and observing the celebration. Despite the costumes, songs, and dance of the *bumba,* the ceremony seems to bore the town leaders as much as it entertains them—especially at the beginning, when they loll passively in their seats and occasionally talk to one another and yawn. However, dos Santos is careful not to allow his audience to be passively entertained. Instead of showing the performance from beginning to end, he intercuts the *bumba-meu-boi* with shots of Fabiano, who is writhing in pain on the floor of the jail cell, and of Sinhá Vitória, who has no idea what has happened to her husband and waits anxiously for him on the church steps.

The technique that dos Santos uses in this sequence, which moves back and forth between the public performance of the symbolic ox slaying and the action of "real" peasants, is reminiscent of Eisenstein's dialectical montage in *Strike* (1924), in which shots of workers being killed by soldiers are intercut with shots of a bull being slaughtered. In *Strike*, the visual metaphor or "associative link" between the different subjects in the montage is the act of butchering. In *Vidas secas*, the link is not killing per se, but rather the idea of power and subservience. In the *bumba* ceremony, the workers serve up themselves and the product of their labor (the ox) to the master. Despite his obsequiousness, Fabiano is served up to the police for punishment because of a purported attack on their authority; Sinhá Vitória waits in anxious silence for Fabiano's return. The sequence is made even more disturbing by the festive *bumba* music that plays as the montage moves from shots of the performers to close-ups of Fabiano in pain to the barely visible figure of Sinhá Vitória, who is waiting with her children in a darkened street. (The socioeconomic and political significance of the *bumba* also extends to two later sequences in the film: the first is a branding scene dos Santos has added to the movie that makes clear the calf being corralled by Fabiano and branded by the landowner is, like the sacrificial ox, the fruit of Fabiano's labor; the second is a scene near the end of the film in which Fabiano is forced to servilely relinquish his horse to the landowner, who is positioned above him on horseback.)

The film dramatizes the imprisonment of Fabiano in a relatively faithful way, but it adds a band of armed men to the action. At one point in the book Fabiano briefly considers joining the *cangaceiros* (bandits) to get back at the yellow soldier who harassed him and then threw him in jail. Like many of Fabiano's thoughts, however, his idea for revenge is fleeting and he does nothing to act upon it. In the film, dos Santos modifies the jail scene to include a young man who helps the injured Fabiano to lie down. No indication of the young man's identity is given until the next morning, when he is revealed to be the godchild of the leader of a band of armed mercenaries. Presumably under the command of a landowner, or "captain," the mercenaries ride into town on horseback, calling at the house of the vicar and demanding the young man's release. The scene is surprising because it reveals subservience on the part of the vicar, the mayor, and Fabiano's landowner boss, all of whom rush to the jail to comply with the armed horseman's demand. When the local landowner notices Fabiano sitting in the cell, he tells the jailer to release him. After his release, Fabiano and his family stop to tend his injuries as they make their way home. The men on horseback approach, and the same young man who helped Fabiano in jail now offers him his horse to ride while he walks behind with Sinhá Vitória and her sons.

Two aspects of this new material are worth consideration: while the armed men succeed in intimidating the town authorities, they also frighten Sinhá Vitória, who moves out of the street and nervously watches their approach. There is absolutely nothing here to suggest that the armed men in any way serve or empower the poor or that they are going to overthrow the ruling class. (Their social function is ambiguous, so that they sometimes resemble bandits and sometimes the paid army of a landowner.) After riding the young man's horse, Fabiano and his family come to a fork in the road, where the young man invites Fabiano to join him, remarking that "the captain pays them well." The next shot is a low-angle close-up of Fabiano, who is photographed on horseback with the young man's rifle in his hand. This is one of several shots in the film that gives an epic dimension to the *vaqueiro*, photographed against the sky in the manner of Eisenstein or Ford. But as Fabiano sits and ponders the young man's invitation, a cowbell rings in the distance. The sound of the bell visibly moves Fabiano, who dismounts and hands the gun and horse's reigns back to the young man. The scene ends as the horsemen continue down one road while Fabiano and his family, who have found Baleia, take the other path.

In the book, Fabiano uses his family and their need of him as an excuse for not carrying out his plan to join the *cangaceiros*. In the film, when Fabiano is given the opportunity to join a group of armed men, he declines because of the cowbell, which indicates his inescapable bond with the land. A later episode in the film reaffirms this bond, but its impact is totally different. Fabiano is searching for a lost calf when he comes face-to-face with the yellow soldier, who is lost in the brush and searching for the road back to town. An entire section in the novel describes Fabiano's thoughts as he draws a small machete and makes threatening gestures at the soldier. The film is quite good in capturing the book's sense of real time, or *la durée*, which heightens the suspense as the two men face one another in the brush, their earlier roles of victim and aggressor now reversed. In the book, Fabiano reluctantly sheathes his machete, having convinced himself that despite the soldier's harassment of him, "the government is the government" (163). The film takes a different approach: Fabiano's wrath toward the soldier is unabated until he hears the bellow of a lost calf. Like the cowbell, the calf's bellow has a clear psychological effect, and Fabiano puts away his machete, subserviently allowing the soldier to pass. His comment, "the government is the government," seems far less convincing here, but once again his immediate and overriding concern is his connection to the land. The film also modifies the book's narrative in less obvious ways. What makes *Vidas secas* different from Ramos's earlier novels is his decision to write about a family of illiterate backlanders who rarely speak even among themselves. Throughout the novel, however, we are made privy to the thoughts of Fabiano, Sinhá Vitória, their two young sons, and even Baleia. Ramos makes considerable use of free indirect discourse—a technique in which a third-person narration simulates an inner monologue or stream of consciousness. A few early reviews of *Vidas secas* took issue with this approach, claiming that Ramos was giving false psychological depth to "rustic" types. Curiously, that the same narrative technique was used to attribute psychological complexity to Baleia seemed less problematic to critics, who apparently could imagine an animal reflecting on the world but had difficulty believing that Fabiano had the intelligence to equate his nomadic existence with that of a wandering Jew.

Through the device of inner speech, Sinhá Vitória is presented early on in the novel as a woman obsessed with owning a decent bed like the one owned by Mr. Tomás, a man for whom Fabiano once worked. In "Sinhá Vitória," she is upset by Fabiano and chastises him for gambling away money that could have been used toward the purchase of materials for the bed. She is equally disturbed by Fabiano's retaliatory comment that she walks like a parrot in the dress shoes that she wears to town. His criticism of her awkward gait evokes in her mind the image of the family's parrot, which she was forced to kill—a painful memory that becomes associated in her mind with Fabiano's gambling and her desire for the comfortable bed. In "The World Covered with Feathers," which appears at the end of the book, Sinhá Vitória notices that certain migratory birds have returned to the *sertão*—the signal of another drought. As Fabiano walks outside with his gun, his thoughts immediately turn to the deceased Baleia, his constant companion on hunts. Sitting on the riverbank, he shoots several birds, picks up their carcasses, and places them in his pack. The memory of Baleia returns as he walks back toward the house. Convinced that his wife's prediction about the significance of the birds is correct, he realizes that his family must pack up their belongings and start their journey across the *sertão* once again.

In the equivalent part of the film, Sinhá Vitória receives somewhat less attention, probably because her character in the book is developed mainly through her thoughts as opposed to her actions. The film shows her cooking in a cramped and darkened kitchen area, complaining about the "miserable" conditions of the small house and Fabiano's gambling. Meanwhile, we can hear Fabiano responding to her complaints from the next room as if he were speaking to himself. He criticizes her shoes and her parrot-like walk and then lies down in his hammock. Sinhá Vitória joins Fabiano in the bedroom, looks out the window, and comments on the ominous presence of the birds. The book's emphasis on Sinhá Vitória's almost obsessive associations between the bed, the shoes, and the dead parrot, which function as correlatives for her misery, are entirely discarded; instead, we merely hear her prophesies about the impending drought. As in the novel, Fabiano gets up, grabs his rifle, walks out of the house, and proceeds to shoot randomly at the birds. The chief difference here is that Baleia is still alive, but that she lies passively in the sun, as opposed to accompanying her master into the brush, is an indication that something is amiss.

Although the film cannot convey each character's complex train of thought in the novel, it is effective in portraying the impact of the birds' arrival on the *retirantes.* (Ramos had initially chosen "O mundo coberto de penas" [The World Covered with Feathers], whose double meaning of *penas* as "feathers" and "pains" emphasizes the misery of life in the *sertão,* to serve as the novel's title.) In a shot that resembles a photograph or freeze frame, Fabiano is shown standing outside the house, while Sinhá Vitória is inside at the window. Both are immobile, looking off-camera. The scene is riveting, partly because of the stillness of the characters and partly because their transfixed gazes are intercut with images of the sun, which grows larger and more brilliant. On the soundtrack we can hear Sinhá Vitória quietly praying as she holds a rosary in her hands. Next we see a close-up of Baleia, who appears equally mesmerized by the intensity of the sun. The stillness is finally broken as the younger son, as if to reaffirm the magnitude of what he sees, raises his arm over his forehead in an attempt to shield his eyes from the glare. This sequence ends with

Fabiano's voice heard off-screen, as if his thoughts were suddenly transformed into speech: "It's going to catch fire."

Following the sequence, dos Santos includes additional shots of a descriptive nature, showing in more concrete ways than in the novel the onset and effects of the drought. In one scene Fabiano is cutting down and burning cactus plants to provide water for his steer; we cut to a shot of a sick cow who can no longer stand, then to a close-up of a dead steer's head covered with flies. Whereas the novel moves immediately from the appearance of the migratory birds to the last chapter, entitled "Fuga" (Flight), the film rearranges events so that the sense of helplessness and doom suggested by the birds and confirmed by the scenes of sick and dead cattle are extended casually into the sequences that show Fabiano relinquishing his cattle and his horse to the landowner, then assuming a threatening and then distracted attitude in his encounter with the yellow soldier, and finally tracking and shooting Baleia. The action then ends as it begins, with the family slowly crossing the *sertão* to the sound of a screeching oxcart wheel. (The sound of this wheel, as Noel Burch has observed, is one of the most effective motifs in the film [98].) Despite a brief exchange between Fabiano and Sinhá Vitória, there is nothing to suggest that their lives will be any different or better. The shot of the *sertão* as they round a fence to begin their journey is so overwhelming in its magnitude and scorched brightness that the question is not whether they will have a better life but whether they will survive the journey at all.

Dos Santos employs an array of cinematic techniques to convey a family that thinks but rarely speaks. Like the book, the film relies heavily on the characters' guttural sounds and gestures to communicate their will or desires. When an exchange does occur, the characters are often filmed from afar or with their backs to the screen so that their words seem to emanate from a source other than themselves. In a few instances dos Santos uses a voice-over as opposed to conventional dialogue; its effect has more the feel of an unspoken thought being overheard by the audience, as in an interior monologue, as opposed to a speech addressed to a character. Examples of these techniques can be seen in the first part of the film. At one point in their journey across the *sertão*, Fabiano and his family take a brief rest; sitting on the ground, Sinhá Vitória looks at the family parrot, which is precariously perched on top of a small trunk that contains the family's possessions. With a pained expression on her face, she grabs the parrot, pulls it struggling and squawking behind the trunk, and winces as she breaks the bird's neck. The next shot shows the body of the parrot plucked clean of feathers and roasting over a small fire as Sinhá Vitória's voice-over explains: "It served nothing. It didn't even know how to talk" (see fig. 6). Her comment is not presented as part of a dialogue or directed to anyone in particular; it is as if we are overhearing her private rationalization for killing the family's pet. As the family continues its journey, Sinhá Vitória and Fabiano see birds circling in the distance. Over a shot of the birds, Sinhá Vitória's off-screen voice says: "I bet there are people over there." Although the status of the voice is ambiguous, it has the quality of a thought being expressed as opposed to a statement directed toward Fabiano. In the next shot, Sinhá Vitória, Fabiano, and their younger son move ahead in the distance, but the camera stays with the older son, who, overcome by heat and lack of food, becomes dizzy and falls down in the middle of the road. In the distance, Fabiano and Sinhá Vitória pause to exchange a few words about the journey, but Sinhá Vitória's back is turned and they are so far removed from the camera that we cannot see them speaking. As they speak, we cut to a close-up of the boy curled up on the road. The parents' words have a strangely disembodied quality—as if what we are hearing is emanating from a displaced diegetic source.

Dos Santos handles the "speech" of Baleia in a very different fashion. In early scenes the dog is shown barking at critical moments: for example, when the older boy falls down, Baleia barks at Fabiano, who then looks back to find his son collapsed on the road. Similarly, after the family discovers an abandoned shack that becomes their temporary home, Baleia barks and runs after a cavy, which she brings back as food for the family. Although we never hear Baleia's thoughts (as we do in the novel), she is in fact the only character in the film whose "speech" is consistently represented in the form of synchronous action and sound; her barks are acknowledged and heeded by the family as if they were actual words. Her vocal interaction with them goes hand-in-hand with the closeness that the family members feel toward her—a closeness greater than they seem to feel among themselves. The scene in which Baleia presents Sinhá Vitória with the cavy is a good example: as Baleia returns from the hunt, Sinhá Vitória runs to her and kisses and licks her blood-covered snout. This moving scene contrasts sharply with the interaction between the

Figure 6. Maria Ribeiro in *Vidas secas*. (Museum
of Modern Art/Film Stills Archive)

family members, especially between Sinhá Vitória and Fabiano, who
rarely speak to one another and are ill at ease with any physical expression of concern, desire, or need. The film captures this unease in a scene
that shows Fabiano and Sinhá Vitória sitting side-by-side on the ground.
Fabiano nudges Sinhá Vitória with his elbow and points to a cloud that
has appeared in an otherwise clear sky. The cloud is a welcome sign, since
it could mean that the drought will soon be over. But there is also the
possibility that the cloud will simply dissipate and that the drought will
continue. In response to Fabiano's nudge, Sinhá Vitória looks worriedly
at the sky. She then draws closer to him and places her hand on his fore-
arm. But after a second or two, she withdraws the hand and pulls back,
sensing the awkwardness of this rare intimate contact.

One of the more unusual attempts to convey internalized, free indirect discourse occurs shortly after this scene. Its source is a brief passage in an episode of the novel entitled "Inverno" (Winter), when the
family is huddled together as winter rains threaten to flood the house.
The boys are unable to sleep because of the loud rain and the sound of
their parents' voices: "It wasn't actually a conversation: they were loose

and drawn-out phrases with repetitions and incongruities. At times a guttural interjection energized the ambiguous speech. In truth neither was paying attention to the other's words: they were projecting images that entered their spirit, and the images followed on from one another and became distorted, without any way of controlling them. Since their verbal resources were few, they tried to remedy the deficiency by speaking loudly" (Graciliano Ramos 94).

Dos Santos moves this incident to the first part of his film, placing it shortly after the family takes refuge in the abandoned house. It begins with Sinhá Vitória commenting on the good quality of the land, which will enable her sons to grow strong—a comment that is heard and acknowledged by Fabiano. This is followed by two elaborated soliloquies, or "ambiguous speeches," by Fabiano and Sinhá Vitória, who often speak simultaneously. The characters turn slightly away from one another as they deliver these speeches, as if their inner preoccupations were being represented in a stylized, presentational form. Dos Santos takes this opportunity to lay bare the central desires and concerns of the two characters. Sinhá Vitória speaks for the first time of Mr. Tomás's bed and of her desire to have one just like it to replace their present bed, which is made of uncomfortable tree branches. (This soliloquy is based on the "Sinhá Vitória" episode of the book.) Fabiano's soliloquy (drawn from a section entitled "Fabiano") expresses his desire to speak Portuguese as well as Mr. Tomás, an educated man who owned a cotton gin but fell victim to the drought because of his preference for reading over attending to his landowner duties.

One might speculate that dos Santos eliminated the novel's description of Fabiano telling a story because it would have added little or nothing to the film, which mainly concentrates on the daily life and external struggles of a *retirante* family. Even literary critics have had little to say about "Winter," which of all the sections in the novel seems the least essential to the development of the narrative. It describes Fabiano in a rare expansive moment recounting certain *façanhas*, or deeds. The winter rains have changed his mood, and his story to the children, which he has apparently told before, becomes exaggerated and even optimistic. We are never told the details of his account; we only know that his sons have difficulty following the story because of the change in tone. The older boy is especially disconcerted:

Unable to see his father's features, he closed his eyes to try to understand him better. But a doubt had surfaced. Fabiano had changed the story—and that diminished its verisimilitude. A disillusion. He stretched and yawned. It would have been better had the words been repeated. He would squabble with his brother in trying to interpret them. He would fight because of the words—and his conviction would grow. Fabiano should have repeated them. But no. A variation had appeared, and the hero had become human and contradictory. (100–101)

To a certain extent this passage functions thematically for the book as a whole. Between and within sections, characters' thoughts and moods often undergo swift, radical changes, revealing their curiosity about language and undermining certain stereotypical notions about "primitives" derived from late nineteenth- and early twentieth-century literature. In fact, Ramos's novel is as much or more concerned with the "human and contradictory" language and consciousness of the *retirante* as it is with the brutal landowning system of the Northeast. By creating characters who have complex, changing psychological needs, fears, and desires, Ramos hoped to elicit greater sympathy for the lives of thousands of families in the Northeast. His personification of Baleia risked sentimentality or bathos, but it, too, ultimately succeeded, drawing readers even closer into the narrative and creating a feeling of empathy that few works of Brazilian literature have achieved.

In this regard, it should be noted that the boy's confusion and curiosity about the story told by his father link the "Winter" episode with "O menino mais velho" (The Oldest Child), a section in which Ramos again raises the issue of language. In this section, the boy hears the unfamiliar word *inferno* spoken by a faith healer named Sinhá Terta. The boy asks his mother to explain the word. Her reference to an "evil place" with "hot spikes" seems insufficient, and he asks her if she has ever seen it. Sinhá Vitória responds to his repeated questioning by hitting him on the head. Crying, he runs out of the house, sits on the ground, and cradles Baleia, who squirms in the boy's too-tight embrace. As he mutters to the dog, his thoughts and feelings jump back and forth between his anger and pain over his mother's punishing response and his attempts to imagine what "hell" must look like.

Dos Santos's film dramatizes this scene in its entirety, but it somewhat plays down the boy's curiosity about words and his desire to understand what he does not know, giving greater emphasis to the ironic relationship between the word *hell* and the boy's immediate surroundings. A subjective camera shows the boy looking at the family's ramshackle house, at the distant hilly terrain, at a strutting chicken, at a few meager cattle, at the blazing sun, and finally at the family house again. A voice-over accompanies several of these shots, and in each instance the boy can be heard uttering the word *inferno* or repeating his mother's phrases *evil place* and *hot spikes.* We then see the boy's face as he repeats over and over the word *inferno.* Dos Santos's use of the subjective camera is an effective alternative to the book's free indirect style; at the same time, however, it pays more attention to the objective surface of the character's world, which is always visibly present. Ultimately, the power of dos Santos's film, which is one of the masterpieces of Brazil's Cinema Novo, lies in its straightforward record of parched nature and grinding poverty.

From Comedy to Allegory: *El justicero, Fome de amor,* and *Azyllo muito louco*

Vidas secas enjoyed great critical success, but dos Santos was forced to return to his job at the *Jornal do Brasil.* Although his stay there was brief, he made two short films for the newspaper: *Um moço de 74 anos* (A Seventy-Four-Year-Old Fellow; 1965) describes the history of the *Jornal do Brasil* since its founding in 1891, and *O Rio de Machado de Assis* (1965) is a tribute to one of Brazil's most admired authors and to nineteenth-century Rio.

In late 1965, dos Santos accepted an invitation to join the Institute for Mass Communication at the newly established University of Brasília. According to Salem, dos Santos never actually relocated to Brasília, preferring to commute between Rio and the newly constructed capital in the interior. The film critic Jean-Claude Bernardet, who was on the faculty at the time, jokes about how the head of the institute tried to keep the upper administration from discovering that dos Santos only occasionally went to classes and held office hours. Despite his erratic presence, dos Santos forged a bond with his students, several of whom would work with him on film projects, such as *Fala Brasília* (Speak Brasília; 1966), a short documentary about immigration to the capital city and the many dialects of Portuguese spoken there. He was also invited to make a documentary for the Kennedy administration's Alliance for Progress, *Cruzada ABC* (ABC Crusade; 1966), which, according to one of dos Santos's associates, was implicitly critical of the alliance, photographing Americans passing out small cans of powdered milk to lines of starving Northeasterners (Salem 201). About this time in 1966, more than a dozen faculty members from the University of Brasília were fired by the right-wing military government that two years earlier had overthrown the civilian presidency of João Goulart. Over two hundred faculty members protested the firings by handing in their resignations—including dos Santos, who found himself out of a job once again. When he was given the opportunity by Condor Filmes to make *El justicero* (The Enforcer; 1967), an urban comedy of manners based on the book *As vidas de el justicero* (The Lives of the Enforcer) by João Bethencourt, dos Santos formed a crew that consisted largely of his former students from the University of Brasília.

El justicero deals with the upper-middle-class society of the Zona Sul in the period immediately following the 1964 military coup, when journalists such as Carlos Heitor Cony were still able to write freely and even poke fun at the military.[10] The main characters are Jorge (Arduíno Colasanti), a playboy who reads Sartre, Marx, and Engels and who, as "el Jus," seeks to defend the rights of the poor and the honor of virgins; Lenine (Emmanuel Cavalcanti), a Marxist who has been contracted by Jorge to write his biography but ends up making a movie about his life; Ana Maria (Adriana Prieto), Jorge's independent-minded girlfriend; and Jorge's father, "El General," a shipping company magnate and general in the army reserves who wants Jorge to fix him up with his girlfriends. Prior to being released, *El justicero* was cut by the censors because of its graphic language. Shortly after it appeared in theaters, all copies were confiscated by the military police. According to dos Santos, the military disliked the film's corrupt obnoxious general who chased young women. As a humorous critique of Rio society, however, the film lampooned not only the military and the Far Right but also the liberal intelligentsia. Consistently irreverent and often praised or denounced as a *brincadeira,* or game, *El justicero* made its mark as the first comedy to be associated with the Cinema Novo movement, which was best known for serious films such as Rocha's *Terra em transe* (Land in Anguish) and

Saraceni's *O desafio* (The Challenge)—both of which were released that same year and had similar difficulties with the censors. *El justicero* also introduced the public to a new leading man, Arduíno Colasanti. A surfer who was discovered in Rio by one of dos Santos's assistants, Colasanti would go on to star in several other films by dos Santos, most notably as the Frenchman Jean in *Como era gostoso o meu francês.*

What dos Santos calls the *besteirol* (silly, nonsensical) aspect of *El justicero* sets the tone for his subsequent even more playful and irreverent films such as *Azyllo muito louco* (A Very Crazy Asylum; 1971) and *Como era gostoso o meu francês.* In this case, the basic plot resembles a screwball comedy except that the central character has a Candide-like naivete and dos Santos uses him for social satire. The opening shot is amusingly self-reflexive: Jorge, Lenine, and the other cast members are seated in a movie theater and ready to view the picture that we are about to see. The camera moves back and forth between the amused faces of the cast members, who call out to the film's opening logo showing a Condor Filmes bird perched on a mountaintop; the bird, as if having heard the shouts and jeers, spreads its wings and flies away. A similar scene is repeated at the end of *El justicero*, when Lenine and Jorge are previewing the film-within-the-film that Lenine has made of Jorge's life. This was the first time that dos Santos used a narrative framing device in a movie, and he would repeat the technique in other films, most notably *O amuleto de Ogum* (The Amulet of Ogum; 1975) and *Tenda dos milagres* (Tent of Miracles; 1977), the latter of which is also based on the idea of a film-within-a-film.

As in dos Santos's later films, *El justicero* makes comic and often ironic use of music. In the second scene, Jorge is stretched out on his bed eating from a platter of food and listening to a bossa nova. The sound system behind him is as up-to-date as the apartment, with its trendy white walls, sixties pop art, and modern furnishings. When Jorge turns off the music, his houseman, who likes looking at *Playboy* and cutting out pictures of women in bathing suits, tells him that *forró* is a far superior music; he puts a record on and begins to dance in the traditional Northeastern style. Jorge tells him to turn off the music, which he clearly dislikes, and to play Vivaldi. The houseman puts on the classical LP, but he (perhaps deliberately) fails to change the speed, and it sounds like a dissonant dirge. After calling the houseman's attention to his carelessness, Jorge goes to the record player himself and changes the speed, whereupon the dirge-like music transforms into a sprightly classical melody.

Another amusing segment involves Lenine, Jorge's biographer, who goes to the beach in the Zona Sul to interview people about "el Jus." Arduíno Colasanti was known as a surfer and the women being interviewed refer to his surfing abilities in addition to his striking good looks. Ironically no one talks about his attributes as the enforcer, and the men seem far less impressed with Jorge than do the women. Equally comic is that in his search for "justice," Jorge rarely finds himself endangered in any way. This is not true of his enforcer companions, who, in one scene, take a beating at the hands of the gang of his adversary, Búfalo, while he remains safely on the sidelines, wooing his newfound love interest, Ana Maria. This confrontation/courtship scene takes place after an especially humorous attempt by Jorge and his followers to preserve the virginity of a young woman to whom Búfalo is attracted. In that episode, Jorge raids a series of apartment buildings looking for the place where Búfalo has taken the young woman. To get past the doormen at the different buildings, he flashes his membership card from the local country club as if it were a police badge. Either because of illiteracy or fear, the doormen believe that he is connected with the police and they give him access to the buildings; on an elevator, one doorman turns to Jorge and asks if the man whom he is seeking is a Communist. When Jorge and his followers finally locate the young woman and Búfalo, the woman is clearly upset that they have interrupted the lovemaking. She throws books and other objects at her so-called rescuers and storms out of the apartment.

Jorge's crusade for justice for women is completely hypocritical. At the same time that he expects women to be virginal and even tries to defend their virginity, as in the scene described above, he has sex with his girlfriends. After a night of intense lovemaking, when he discovers that Ana Maria is not the virgin that he thought she was, he becomes enraged and tells Lenine that she is nothing more than a *puta* (prostitute). Lenine tells Jorge that he is out of sync with the times and that women are no longer expected to be virgins. When Jorge later discovers that Ana Maria is pregnant, he proposes to her out of a sense of obligation, but Ana Maria's reluctance is another sign of the changing times. She finally agrees to marriage, but only after Jorge's father convinces her that marriage is not necessarily sacrosanct and that Jorge can always make other arrangements later on. This scene in the film follows a near fight between Jorge's and Ana Maria's fathers over Ana Maria's pregnancy. After Ana Maria agrees to the marriage, the two men, who were at each other's throat, embrace as if nothing untoward had ever happened.

The film ends with Lenine and Jorge in a screening room. Lenine tells him that the film, like Jorge's life, is banal when compared with the problems of the nation, and when Jorge inquires about an ending, Lenine responds: "Who cares if you marry her or not?" Jorge continues to demonstrate a puritanical and totally alienated demeanor, responding to his filmmaker-chronicler, "I do."

In her biography of dos Santos, Salem comments that dos Santos was reluctant to talk much about *El justicero*. Perhaps this is because the only copy of the film that survived the ban is a bad 16 mm print. In an interview with Tunico Amancio published in 1999, dos Santos gives a short list of problems with the film beyond those encountered with the censors: "First there was the title in Portuñol [a neologism to describe the mixture of Spanish and Portuguese in the title of the book that he adapted]. The actors Arduíno Colasanti and Adriana Prieto were unknown to the public and everyone wondered: is it a Mexican film or an Italian film? It also didn't receive any publicity" (42). But he also conceded that, despite the physical flaws in the copy that survived, the film was extremely funny and worth seeing again.

Immediately following the disappointing public reception and ban of *El justicero,* dos Santos received a grant from the U.S. State Department to spend two months visiting film schools and studios in the United States. Before leaving for the States, he reluctantly accepted a new project based on a story by Guilherme de Figueiredo entitled "História para se ouvir de noite" (Story to be Heard at Night) about two couples who live on an island: Mariana, a concert pianist; Felipe, a painter; Ula, a great beauty; and her husband, Alfredo, a former military officer who is blind and deaf and cannot speak. Dos Santos undertook the project upon his return from the United States, retaining the story's basic premise about four people and a dog living in an isolated place, but changing the title to *Fome de amor: Você nunca tomou banho de sol inteiramente nua?* (Hunger for Love: Have You Never Sunbathed Completely Naked?; 1967) and using Figueiredo's plot about relationships and infidelity to tell an allegorical tale about the sixties counterculture and the frustrated attempts by left-wing radicals to effect social change. The most interesting aspect of the film is his uncharacteristic use of discontinuous editing, which he says was inspired by the French New Wave as well as by the American underground filmmakers Stan Brakhage and Jonas Mekas, whom he met during his visit to the United States: "'[The film involves] a much more liberal treatment of time than [what I had filmed] before,'" he remarks. "'The idea [was to create a sense of] visual memory, everything that rolls around in one's head. This film closely identified with the trip [to the United States]; it was the result of that trip'" (qtd. in Amancio 47).

When dos Santos was asked why there was no organized protest against the government's confiscation of *El justicero,* he replied that neither he nor anyone else dared to complain. The 1968 coup within the military shifted power even further to the right and in the new atmosphere of violent repression people were afraid to make any statement against the regime. On December 13, 1968, a new law was enacted (AI-5) that suspended individual rights; anything cultural or artistic that failed to comply with the regime's National Security Law was deemed suspicious and therefore illegal (Ramos and Miranda 114). A reign of terror targeted left-wing intellectuals and student groups; arrests, imprisonments, and the torture of "subversives" were commonplace for the next few years. Despite *Fome de amor*'s leftist theme, which includes references (sometimes in Spanish) to guerrilla warfare and the Cuban Revolution, it managed to get by the censors. Perhaps they were confused by the film's discontinuous, self-referential style, and perhaps they were oblivious to its use of symbols and allegory.[11]

During this period many Brazilian intellectuals, including the younger generation of filmmakers whose movies aggressively attacked the status quo, went into exile to escape government reprisals. Their low-budget cinema, often self-described as "marginal," featured criminals, prostitutes, and others from the least-known sectors of Brazilian society. Among those who left Brazil after 1968 were the popular musicians Gilberto Gil and Caetano Veloso, the leaders of the Tropicália movement, who had been arrested and briefly put in jail for their protest lyrics. Dos Santos also went into exile, although he never left Brazil. Instead, he and his actors and crew set up shop in the remote coastal town of Parati located south of Rio, where he shot his next three films—the first of which, *Azyllo muito louco*, was based loosely on Machado de Assis's 1888 satirical novella *O alienista* (The Psychiatrist).

O alienista is an ironic tale about the cracks and faults in the foundation of medical science and, in a larger sense, about the potential absurdity of a certain kind of rationality. A psychiatrist, Simão Bacamarte (a name that means "blunderbuss") arrives from Europe to work in the Brazilian coastal town of Itaguaí, where he applies scientific theories learned abroad to determine who among the citizenry is insane and will require institutionalization in his newly constructed asylum, called the Casa Verde, or Green House. Bacamarte and his deferential wife, Dona Evarista, receive backing from the local vicar. Eventually, however, the government, the vicar, and Bacamarte come under attack by an outraged citizenry, whose leader, a barber called Porfírio, seizes control of the town. Following the popular revolt, Porfírio proposes an alliance with Bacamarte, who can help him secure his political hold. Bacamarte therefore continues to experiment with his theories under the leadership of Porfírio and, as a result of shifting political coalitions, the whole town at one point or another becomes a resident of the asylum. When all his scientific theories about sanity versus insanity fail to cohere, Bacamarte concludes that he alone is insane and commits himself, becoming the sole occupant of the Green House.

Critics often complain that despite the fact that he was a mulatto, Machado de Assis never confronted racial prejudice or spoke out against slavery (which was finally abolished in Brazil in 1888). Works such as *O alienista* prove this charge to be false. In the novella, Machado satirizes the vogue of scientific positivism at the end of the nineteenth century, which was often used to classify and subordinate one race or ethnicity over another. The story is not only a subtle critique of science-based ideology but also a commentary on political beliefs and alliances; it was published at a time when Brazil was on the verge of becoming a republic after centuries of monarchial rule. There is little doubt that the political coalitions and divisions described in the novella are allegorical representations of the actual political swings and shifts of the day.

As in his previous film, dos Santos also chose to speak allegorically, and *Azyllo muito louco* could easily be incorporated into what Ismail

Xavier describes as the Brazilian tendency or movement in the late sixties and early seventies to produce films on the order of "national allegories" (*Alegorias*). *Azyllo muito louco* emphasizes the institutional Green House, which functions as a metaphor for the country as a whole under the new military regime. In creating what he calls a "very loose" adaptation of Machado's work, dos Santos decided to merge two characters from the story, the vicar and the scientist, into a single individual. Dos Santos explains that by making Bacamarte (Nildo Parente) a psychiatrist-priest, he was able to cut down on the number of cast members; more importantly, he gave Bacamarte not only rational but also moral and spiritual authority to wield power (Salem 249). Still other changes were made: Bacamarte becomes the religious advisor of Dona Evarista (Isabel Ribeiro), a powerful woman who is married to Porfírio (Arduíno Colasanti), a wealthy plantation owner and town leader. Bacamarte's mission is to "decolonize" the minds of the citizenry of a town called Serafim, giving them a sense of their importance and strength as a people. He later decides to treat the ostensibly more powerful members of the community who, in his view, experience delusions of grandeur. To attack the first "neurosis," he places all the poor people in the asylum. Instead of being upset by their incarceration, the poor rejoice because they no longer have to work for food and shelter. When the local economy begins to suffer because of their internment, Bacamarte reverses himself and places all the rich and powerful, including Porfírio and Dona Evarista, in the Green House. In one of her delusionary moments, Dona Evarista proclaims that she will transform Serafim into a new and beautiful city that will become the site for the great industries of the future. Bacamarte's cure for Dona Evarista's flight of fancy constitutes one of the more darkly humorous moments in the movie; it consists of her repeating over and over "There is no country poorer than this one."

Azyllo muito louco is dos Santos's first period film, although the sets and costumes by Luís Carlos Ripper seem designed less with the intent of authenticating a particular era than with giving the film an unusual, anachronistic look. For example, the diminutive town crier who announces the arrival of Bacamarte to Serafim at the beginning of the movie is dressed in a colorful and flamboyant costume that looks more like the Mad Hatter's from *Alice in Wonderland* than a nineteenth-century public servant's. Bacamarte's arrival on the shores of Serafim, where he is greeted by Dona Evarista and other social bigwigs, is treated less like a solemn ceremony to greet a religious leader than like a carnival (see fig. 7). All the characters are dressed in brilliantly colored costumes; Dona Evarista and Bacamarte are carried into town on bright red litters. In a later scene, as Bacamarte listens to the confessions of the townspeople, the camera moves out of the church to focus on the long line of people who are waiting to have an audience with the priest; one outfit looks like something out of *Thousand and One Nights,* and several characters wear bizarre conical hats.

Azyllo muito louco is also dos Santos's first color film—a decision based on Brazilian theater owners' new reluctance to exhibit black-and-white movies. There is no question that filming in color enhances the costumes and settings, which play an important role in the film; yet according to dos Santos, Brazil did not have then, nor does it have now, the proper laboratories or technical ability to manipulate color in the post-production phase so that images acquire a specific tone or palette. *Azyllo muito louco* looks as good as it does chiefly because of the basic stock, an inexpensive German brand called Orwo, which makes the blues look dark and tends to give a red hue or tint to the rest of the spectrum (Amancio 50).

Unlike his earlier movies, which rely on neorealist techniques, *Azyllo muito louco* is a highly stylized production filled with elaborate costumes. The emphasis on political critique remains constant, although in a far more indirect fashion. In essence, the film is a commentary on the way in which Brazil, similar to the fictional town of Serafim, has undergone a number of "treatments" by different political authorities whose social and economic "cures" are often carried out with assistance from abroad. According to dos Santos, the 1968 coup is the main inspiration for the movie. As he wryly remarked in an interview in *O globo* at the time, "'There was always someone who thought they could save Brazil with a bunch of formulas'" (qtd. in Salem 249), such as the much-touted right-wing "economic miracle" that devastated the country. The film is exuberant in its tongue-in-cheek humor and satire, which is largely directed at public officials, and in its offbeat or just slightly out-of-tune characterizations. The performances often verge on the surreal—as can be seen in the final shot, in which Bacamarte, now the sole resident of

Figure 7. The arrival of Simão Bacamarte (Nildo Parente) on the shores of Serafim in *O alienista*. (Cinemateca Brasileira, São Paulo)

the Green House, conducts a nonexistent orchestra outdoors. The strangeness of the actors' gestures and dialogue is also heightened by the film's elliptical form. But the otherworldly atmosphere is created largely by the settings, costumes, and performers, who seem less like actors in a movie and more like figures on a stage playing out an elaborate improvisation. The atonal music score by Guilherme Magalhães Vaz adds to this strangeness, giving a disturbing and anachronistic character to the beautiful images. The music frequently and purposely overpowers what the characters are saying, making the dialogue totally incomprehensible. In its total effect, this is one of dos Santos's most Brechtian movies, relying on devices of alienation and estrangement that bring a coded political satire to the fore.

Like *Fome de amor*, *Azyllo muito louco* surprised both moviegoers and the critics. The film is so different from dos Santos's earlier works and so difficult at times to follow that the general public had only a vague notion of what it was about—let alone an understanding of its political implications. In fact, the film is so subtle in its critique of authoritarianism that the censors permitted its release without demanding a single change. Although it did not do well at the box office, it was selected to compete at the Cannes Film Festival and was reviewed favorably in *Le monde.* Among those who especially appreciated *Azyllo muito louco*'s style and politics were Spanish film critics, who praised its "new aesthetic." Perhaps because this aesthetic was reminiscent of a surrealist master, *Azyllo muito louco* was awarded the Cannes Film Festival prize named in honor of Buñuel.

Culture and Cannibalism: *Como era gostoso o meu francês*

Following the ultraconservative crackdown in 1968, the political implications of dos Santos's film adaptations became increasingly more oblique and allegorical. There was a certain tension or ambiguity in his choice of projects: the Brazilian government was less likely to censor his adaptations of classics (particularly when they were aimed at an intellectual or art-movie audience), and through them it could acquire a liberal aura or a degree of cultural capital, not only by allowing them to be produced, but also by providing (in some cases) financial backing. At the same time, dos Santos was able to use respected literature to comment on government policies. Nowhere was his strategy more evident than in his adaptation of *O alienista,* which was released at a moment when the military was sending hundreds of citizens to prison for "subversive" activities.

Shortly after *Azyllo muito louco,* dos Santos directed his most interesting film of the period, *Como era gostoso o meu francês,* which is based not on a novel but on the German explorer Hans Staden's celebrated sixteenth-century chronicle *Brasilien: Die wahrhaftige Histoire der wilden, nacken, grimmigen Menschenfresser-Leute* (Brazil: The True History of the Wild, Naked, Fierce, Man-Eating People; 1557), in which he describes his capture by the cannibalistic Tupinambá when he was living among the Portuguese in the area now known as Rio de Janeiro. According to Salem, dos Santos had long been contemplating a film project about Staden's adventure and about the roughly contemporary formation of a Huguenot community on an island in Guanabara Bay that the director passed every day on his regular commute from Niterói to Rio (258). But dos Santos's imagination was also fired by newspaper accounts of the plight of an indigenous community in the Northeast with which he had contact when making *Vidas secas*. As a result of the Brazilian government's attempt to bring "civilization" to the interior, an entire culture was on the verge of extinction. This situation harked back to the first encounters between Europeans and Brazil's native inhabitants; in particular, dos Santos was reminded of one of the earliest colonial records describing the decimation by Portuguese troops of a tribe known as the Caetés, who had killed and eaten a shipwrecked Portuguese bishop. His film would therefore use Staden's text for its basic plot but would also treat a whole tradition of colonial discourse and ethnographic representation as if it were present-day news. In the process, the film would become less a "translated" adaptation of Staden's work than a subversive retelling of his story; it would treat the native populations of the sixteenth century in realistic fashion, but it would ultimately be an experiment in pastiche and intertextuality, offering a political satire about global capitalism and the Brazilian economic "miracle" of the 1960s and 1970s.

In one sense, every film adaptation can be understood as a type of intertextuality or pastiche, if only because the very process of adaptation involves deliberate imitation. But *Como era gostoso o meu francês* has a more complicated relation to its sources than the usual movie based on a book. It draws on a wide range of other historical narratives besides Staden's and at various junctures it becomes a stylistic hodgepodge: realistic images of Tupinambá life, photographed in documentary fashion on vibrant color stock, are mixed with elements of obvious burlesque, and dramatic reenactments are interspersed with title cards quoting directly from sixteenth-century sources. The film's use of colonial history is particularly dense and layered, revealing contradictions in the sources. Throughout, it suggests that the historical archive is as riven by conflict as contemporary politics, and it makes clear that the country's past and present-day realities are not distinct. Although the major historical trauma it exposes is a familiar one of European domination and genocide, it suggests that this irreducible violence keeps returning and repeating itself in the here and now; meanwhile, it converts the traumatic event described in Staden's text—the cannibalistic act—into a provocative metaphor for resistance to a modern society of global capital and foreign consumption.

We can appreciate the complexity of dos Santos's treatment of historical narrative if we examine the brief precredit sequences of the film, which are based on the same events that Claude Lévi-Strauss once remarked upon: "At this point, history took such a strange turn that I am surprised that no novelist or scenario-writer has yet made use of it. What a marvelous film it would make!" (83). On the soundtrack, we hear a narrator's voice reading from a sixteenth-century text—not by Staden, but by the French admiral Durand de Villegaignon, in a famous letter addressed to the Protestant leader John Calvin, about the religious community Villegaignon had established in 1555 off the coast of Rio. A recent convert, Villegaignon had written to Calvin in 1557 asking him to send missionaries to the island, which was to become a religious haven for Catholics and Protestants alike. But just as the island experiment got underway, fierce theological debates broke out. The arguments were exacerbated by Villegaignon's tyrannical leadership—not to mention the daily hardships caused by unfamiliar surroundings, food shortages, disease, and the constant threat of attack by the Portuguese. Villegaignon finally drove out the Protestant missionaries. Lacking material support from the indigenous Brazilian population, whom he considered "beasts with human faces," and with the Portuguese pressing for control, Villegaignon ultimately abandoned Fort Coligny, which then came under Portuguese rule in 1560.

Dos Santos's use of Villegaignon's document is blatantly ironic. The original text, written in the formal style of a sixteenth-century epistle, is read by an off-screen announcer delivering the "Latest News from Terra Firme." The text vilifies the local inhabitants, but on the screen we see richly colored images of the Indians behaving hospitably to the Europeans. The text also expresses a good deal of concern about tribal "sin" and "carnal lust," while we clearly see that the European explorers are trying to obtain sexual gratification from the naked Tupinambá women. (The Europeans cover up the women's nakedness with oversized frilly shirts, and then the women run along the crest of a hill, brandishing the shirts over their heads or tossing them away.) At one point the announcer reads Villegaignon's account of a conspirator who, freed of his chains and allowed to plead his case, escaped and drowned in the sea; on the screen, the conspirator is instead bound with a ball and chain, prayed over by a priest, and summarily pushed off a hillside into the ocean. As the "broadcast" continues, scenes of exploitation and murder are accompanied by a Mozart French horn concerto that was the popular soundtrack for the short newsreel "Atualidades francesas" (French Current Events) shown in Brazilian movie theaters in the sixties (Salem 259).

In separate studies of the film, the critics Richard Peña and Randal Johnson observe that this opening prepares us for a film that will consistently challenge official history. For Peña, the quotations from Villegaignon are "ironic, 'historical' counterparts to the events depicted" (193). Johnson agrees, arguing that the film places "quotations of historical documents" in "ironic if not contradictory" relation to the truth (*Cinema* 193). The film's technique, however, is more complicated than this, involving something other than an opposition between lying "history" and transparent "reality." Despite their sly humor and evident irony, the images we see on the screen are no less "historical" than the off-screen voice on the soundtrack; in fact, they derive from a series of well-known texts that are roughly contemporary with Villegaignon's that describe what the historian Philip P. Boucher refers to as "Villegaignon's much publicized Brazilian fiasco" (22)—his appalling rule and the failure of the island colony experiment that has long been part of the official record in Brazil and France. By juxtaposing Villegaignon's letter with a visible enactment of his tyranny, the film might be said to "adapt" a celebrated eyewitness account by the French Huguenot Jean de Léry, whose *Histoire dun voyage fait en la terre du Bresil autrement dite Amerique* (History of a Voyage to the Land of Brazil, Otherwise Called America; 1578) includes a transcription of Villegaignon's letter followed by a denunciation of Villegaignon and a description of his cruel treachery. (In his book, Léry also criticizes the Franciscan André Thevet, who in his *Cosmographie universelle* [Universal Cosmography; 1575], based on his brief stay in the community, sides with Villegaignon in the island religious wars and accuses the Calvinists of intrigue.) Indeed, the scene showing the Indian women swinging the frilly European shirts over their heads comes directly from Léry's account.

Perhaps the best way of explaining the film's opening would be to say that it is made up of two or more historical documents in ironic juxtaposition (framed by a burlesque newsreel) and that it favors one document over the others by granting it the status of photographic "truth." At any rate, it would be a mistake to view *Como era gostoso o meu francês* as a straightforward attempt to mock the archival record. Certainly it mocks historical personages (all of them European), but on one level it is a fairly respectful attempt to adapt or interpret historical narratives. The film is formed by a subtle and dense interweaving of materials toward which dos Santos has a mixed attitude—and no wonder, because these materials are self-contradictory and contradict each other.

In interviews, dos Santos has spoken repeatedly of his use of historical sources to provide as accurate an account as possible of the period.[12] (In addition to Staden, who provides the *donne* for the plot, the film quotes and explicitly identifies various writers in the intertitles—among them the Huguenot Léry, the Franciscan Thevet, the Jesuits Manuel da Nóbrega and José de Anchieta, the early chronicler Pero de Magalhães Gândavo, and the country's first governor-general, Mem de Sá.) Dos Santos recognizes that all the sources are individual interpretations of their period. The film uses them to help reconstruct a bygone era, but it also constructs its own interpretation. As dos Santos states, "'The reality portrayed had disappeared. I had to reconstruct the long-ago past, which implied a personal interpretation of History. I respected all the data available about the Tupinambá culture. As for the relations between the Indians and the French, they were evidently subjected to what I always felt about the question'" (qtd. in Salem 266–67). In other words, *Como era gostoso o meu francês* offers not so much a denunciation of history as a new reading of historic sources adapted as a quasi-documentary narrative about the encounter between cultures.

In *Brasilien* Staden recounts two separate voyages, the first in 1547 and the second in 1549. During the second expedition, Staden became friends with Portuguese settlers and their Tupiniquim allies, helping them fortify their coastal enclave against attacks by roving French troops and their allies, the Tupinambá. While aiding the Portuguese, Staden was captured by the Tupinambá, who believed he was Portuguese. According to Staden, his faith in God and good luck enabled him to endure his months of captivity. They also helped him avoid execution and consumption by the Indians, who came to believe he possessed magical powers when he correctly predicted an enemy attack and later "cured" an ailing tribal chief. Held in captivity for nearly a year, he escaped on a French ship in 1554—just months prior to Villegaignon's arrival.

Among several liberties dos Santos takes with Staden's book is to make the film's captive-protagonist a Frenchman and member of the Villegaignon community. Suspected of conspiring against the French leader, he is the character who appears in the film's opening sequence in ball and chain and is pushed off the hillside into the sea. After a lengthy credit sequence, he is shown struggling with the ball and chain to reach land, where he is first captured by the Portuguese and Tupiniquim, who are enemies of the French, then by the Tupinambá, who mistake him for a Portuguese. Both the Staden account and the film emphasize the mistaken identity, but the former describes at some length Staden's efforts to convince the Tupinambá that he is a German national and a "relative" of the French. By introducing the film with Villegaignon's letter, by incorporating the music of the sixties French newsreel, and by making his protagonist a Frenchman named Jean as opposed to a German named Hans, dos Santos focuses on a nation and culture that, ironically, have constituted a greater influence on the nation than did the actual colonizing power, Portugal, which ousted the French from Brazil in the mid-sixteenth century. Despite Brazil's status as a Portuguese colony until the early nineteenth century, its cultural and intellectual life after 1822 was far more profoundly influenced by France—indeed French was the primary language used in Brazilian schools until quite late in the twentieth century.

When Jean (Arduíno Colasanti) is captured with the Portuguese, the Tupinambá order them all to speak to verify their nationality. One by one, the Portuguese captives recite recipes from cookbooks—an unexpectedly amusing moment that contributes to the motif of eating while reinforcing a comic Brazilian stereotype of the Portuguese as a people obsessed with food. Jean's words in French are vividly different and they puzzle the Tupinambá. (His words, "The savage walks naked and we walk unrecognized," echo Montaigne's sentiments as expressed in "On Cannibals"; 1580) Although the Tupinambá believe he is Portuguese, they do not kill and eat him because of his demonstrated expertise with the small cannon—an expertise that, later in the film, he uses on behalf of the Tupinambá against the Tupiniquim and that gives him a false sense of security and superiority over his captors.

As in Staden's book, the film introduces an old French trader (Manfredo Colasanti) who is regarded as a friend in the Tupinambá village and who agrees to speak with Jean to determine his true nationality. In contrast to Staden's account, however, the film is quite cynical in its depiction of this character. The trader in the film immediately knows that Jean is French, but he tells the Tupinambá that their captive is an enemy. Jean is furious when he realizes what the trader has done, but the trader promises to rescue him on a later visit if, in the meantime, he will help collect commercially valuable wood and pepper. Jean agrees, but only when the trader leaves him some kegs of gunpowder. Upon the trader's return to the village, Jean tells him of his discovery of gold coins among the Indians, and he uses this find as leverage to ensure his freedom. Unfortunately, in the process of digging up Jean's hidden cache of treasure, the two men begin to quarrel over its ownership. Jean kills the trader with a shovel blow to the back of his head and then buries him in the hole that once contained the gold.

There is nothing like this brutal miniature version of *The Treasure of the Sierra Madre* (1948) in Staden's text, in which all violent acts are committed by the Indians. Indeed, the purported savagery of the indigenous population is made all the more vivid to Staden's readers because his book contains a series of woodcuts showing Indians in various stages of anthropophagy. Dos Santos presents thirty-two of these xylographic images as the backdrop for the long credit sequence that follows the Villegaignon opening (see fig. 8). Particularly striking is a woodcut of legs and arms drying on top of a large rack; another depicts a man's head with open eyes on a platter. Perhaps most unsettling of all is a picture of women and children eating body parts that look like fingers or phalluses. Accompanying the sequence is a soundtrack consisting of steady drumbeats and whoops and cries that most moviegoers would associate with Hollywood Indians on the "warpath." It therefore seems ironic that the most explicitly violent act in *Como era gostoso o meu francês* is Jean's attack on the trader. Compared with this cowardly and desperate killing, anthropophagy in the film is presented as a serious and civilized ritual; it, too, involves a blow to the victim's head, but the blow is administered face-to-face, and the ritual requires the victim to face the executioner and call out, "When I die, my friends will come to avenge me." The emphasis in the anthropophagic act, at least as the film treats it, is on heroism and blood vengeance. Far from being a casual or indiscriminate practice, it is reserved for specific individuals who are both

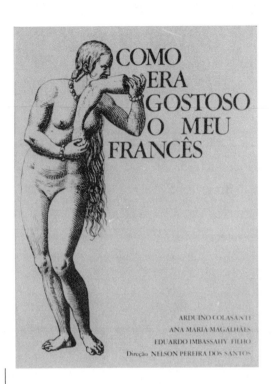

COMO
ERA
GOSTOSO
O MEU
FRANCÊS

ARDUINO COLASANTI
ANA MARIA MAGALHÃES
EDUARDO IMBASSAHY FILHO
Direção NELSON PEREIRA DOS SANTOS

Figure 8. An advertise-
ment for the Brazilian
release of *Como era
gostoso o meu
francês*. (Helena
Salem collection)

symbolically and literally ingested. By contrast, the deadly encounter
between the two Frenchmen is internecine, based on mutual suspicion
and proto-capitalist greed.

Staden's text also differs markedly from the film because it is filled
with references to Christianity. In *Brasilien* Staden frequently prays for
his safety and recites verses from the Bible to calm his growing fears of
execution. At one point, he threatens the Tupinambá warriors with vengeance from his angry God; almost immediately, as if by a miracle, one
Indian who has taunted him most vigorously suddenly falls ill and dies.
Later, Staden is asked to come to the aid of an ailing chief and his family by praying to the European God; seeing an opportunity, he strikes a

bargain with the tribe and agrees to pray on the condition that his own safety is guaranteed. Sure enough, the chief survives, and the legend grows that Staden has magical powers. When a cross he has placed outside his hut is stolen and used for firewood, a powerful storm erupts; when the chief's son erects a new cross in its place, the storm subsides. "Everyone was amazed," Staden writes, "believing that my God did everything that I wanted" (133).

By contrast with this figure, who is both religious and deceitful, Jean in the film is relatively emotionless and at no time demonstrates religiousness. Jean's faith in his survival rests not in God but in the power of commodities (gunpowder and gold), as well as in his technological expertise. Somewhat like Staden, however, Jean plays on the Indians' belief system. He feigns an ability to produce gunpowder out of sand, and he accompanies the Tupinambá into battle, where he fires a cannon against the Tupiniquim. So great is his sense of confidence with respect to his position in the community that at one point he equates himself with Mair, the god who taught the Indians about fire, food, and weapons. But just as Mair was finally rejected by the Tupinambá for his arrogance, so too is Jean, whose every effort to define his individuality and superiority is eventually undercut and punished.

Where the book and film diverge most dramatically is in the representation of women. In Staden's book, the protagonist is chaste (so far as we can determine), and women are described in strictly collective terms. Shortly after Staden is captured, he is taken to a village, where a group of women lead him by a cord around his neck and perform a dance. Soon afterward, the women shave off his eyebrows, beat him, and, despite his vigorous protests, cut off his beard with a pair of French scissors. In subsequent episodes of the book, these and other women are mentioned occasionally, but they recede into the background while the narrative concentrates on Staden's relationships with the male tribe leaders. The film, on the other hand, portrays the early dance scene (depilation occurs later) and then goes on to tell quite another story. Shortly after proclaiming that Jean would be killed on the eighth moon, the leader of the tribe (Eduardo Imbassahy Filho) announces that Seboipep (Ana Maria Magalhães), the widow of his brother, will serve Jean until he is put to death. From this point on, the film pays a great deal of attention to the developing relationship between Jean and Seboipep.

Jean initially rejects Seboipep's attempts to sleep with him in a hammock, but eventually she lives with him like a wife, teaching him the ways of her community.

Here we encounter another of the film's sources or intertexts: *Iracema* (1865), one of Brazil's most cherished nineteenth-century novels about the colonization process. Written by José de Alencar, *Iracema* describes the arrival in Brazil of Martim, the first Portuguese colonizer in northern Ceará; his encounter with the Tabajara tribe; and his attraction to the chief's daughter, Iracema, the "honey-lipped maiden," whose name is an anagram for America. When he arrives in Brazil, Martim is told that Iracema, the designated "virgin of Tupã," guards the secret of her tribe's well-being. Later, in one of the most sensuous chapters of the novel, Iracema climbs into Martim's hammock while he is sleeping and makes love to him. As a result of this act, she can no longer function as the protector of her community and she abandons her family to go off with Martim. Soon afterward, the Tabajara are decimated by an enemy tribe. Iracema dies of grief, but she leaves behind a son, Moacir, who represents a union between the two races.

Alencar's *bon sauvage* creations, including the equally popular *O Guarani* (1857), a novel describing an encounter between an Indian warrior and a European maiden, took on mythical importance during a period of nationalistic fervor in Brazil, when the Indian came to symbolize the country's heritage. The Indian population, of course, had largely disappeared by the nineteenth century thanks to colonial wars and diseases brought by Europeans. Nonetheless, so popular were the writings of Alencar and so powerful were his characterizations of the "noble savage" that Brazilians took increasing pride in their indigenous heritage—at least to the point of giving their children Indian names. The modernist movement of the early twentieth century, which was also steeped in nationalism, perpetuated the same romanticized view of the Indian as hero-symbol by playfully insisting that Brazilians adopt a metaphorical anthropophagism—which, in the eyes of one of the movement's chief proponents, Oswald de Andrade, was one way to counter cultural imperialism. As Robert Stam observes: "Inverting the binary pair of civilization and barbarism in favor of barbarism, Modernism articulated cannibalism as an anticolonialist metaphor in its 'Cannibalist Reviews' and Anthropophagic Manifestoes. . . . The idea was to ingest all foreign techniques and models in order to forge a new synthesis that could be turned against the foreigner" (237). Even though *antropofagismo* was itself an imported model from Europe, Stam points out that "only in Brazil did it become a key trope in a cultural movement that was to prolong itself over many decades" (238). Andrade's representation of the Indian as a symbolic defender of the nation's culture influenced a number of major authors, including Mário de Andrade and Raul Bopp, whose fiction and poetry in the twenties and thirties portrayed the Indian in unexplored and often fantasmagoric ways.

Como era gostoso o meu francês appropriates these familiar conventions of Brazilian narratives about the colonial period, but it provides a fascinating counterpart to the romanticized Indian. Unlike the "romance" between Martim and Iracema, the encounter between Jean and Seboipep is not idealized. Jean shows absolutely no interest in Seboipep, who is not a virgin and whose name in Tupi means "bloodsucker" (Salem 259); in fact, he altogether rejects her amorous advances until his conversation with the French trader, who counsels him to follow the tribe's customs and take advantage of the situation for profit-making purposes. In one of the most sensuous scenes in the film, when the two are playing in the water, the eroticism is cut short by Jean's discovery of a gold coin in Seboipep's navel (see fig. 9). Because gold, unlike gunpowder and firearms, has no commercial value to the Tupinambá, Seboipep tells Jean about gold pieces in a burial ground—which, in turn, leads him to conspire with and then murder the French trader. Shortly after the killing, Jean nearly makes his escape with the treasure by paddling a canoe toward a passing ship. As he makes his way to the ship, he sees Seboipep watching him from the shoreline. In what at first seems like a passage out of Alencar, he paddles back to shore to take her with him. But unlike Iracema, who sacrificed her people to be with Martim, Seboipep refuses to go with Jean; by the time he returns to the canoe, the ship has disappeared from sight. Later in the film, when he tries to escape with his treasure, she shoots him in the leg with an arrow and he discovers to his surprise and dismay that she has chopped a giant hole in the bottom of his canoe. When Jean somewhat plaintively asks her if she intends to make a meal of him, a close-up shows her with a Mona Lisa smile. She calls him her "little neck," which refers to the prize morsel that would be given to her as the captive's wife/keeper. As the

Figure 9. Arduíno
Colasanti as Jean and
Ana Maria Magalhães
as Seboipep in *Como
era gostoso o meu
francês*. (Helena
Salem collection)

film draws to an end, we see her contentedly gnawing on this very morsel. Unlike Iracema, Seboipep survives her encounter with the colonizer and has no offspring with him. On the contrary, she appears quite pleased when Jean's execution day arrives, as if she were looking forward to his final "integration" into the community.

Dos Santos does not end the film on this comic-satiric note, since to do so would be as much a historical distortion as the sentimental endings in Alencar's fiction. As the camera backs away from Seboipep to show a panoramic view of the community, a final quote appears on the screen. The words are from Mem de Sá, the governor-general of Brazil, who wrote in 1557: "There I fought on the sea, so that no Tupiniquim remained alive. The dead stretched rigidly along the shoreline, covering nearly a league." The sudden appearance of the quote is shocking. The film as a whole has made the indigenous world look relatively vibrant, harmless, and healthy, but we are told that Jean's death (like the Portuguese bishop's death in actual history) will eventually be avenged by a mass extermination, carried out by the Portuguese. The quote is particularly unsettling given that during the period in which the film is set, the Tupiniquim were the wartime allies of the Portuguese. As Salem points out, all the values of the historical sources are undermined by the film's conclusion, which underlines the sheer brutality of the Europeans:

> The truth (visualized) of the colonized is counterposed by the ethnocentric view of the European colonizer, who is unable (and does not try) to comprehend an unknown and different culture from his own, and who is merely concerned with conquering it. On the one hand, the Indians marvel at the technological superiority of the Europeans (gunpowder, presents) and they bow in the face of that technology. . . . On the other hand, they remain faithful to their own culture, eating the European seen as the enemy, regardless of how good natured he reveals himself to be. The Indians live a natural and free existence, without sin. . . . And if the Indians kill and eat a few whites considered as enemies, the whites exterminate thousands and thousands of Indians, as Mem de Sá attests in the final quote. Who then are *"les barbares"*? (261)

One of the most important functions of the quote from Mem de Sá is to remind Brazilian audiences that their national identity, even down to the present day, has depended upon the continued extermination of the "New World's" original inhabitants. At the time *Como era gostoso o meu francês* was made, the Brazilian government was in the midst of a drive to uproot indigenous communities in the interior who were in the path of the TransAmazon highway; these people were not only being physically uprooted but also violently forced to become "modern." For dos Santos, the cultural encounter begun in the 1500s was far from over. If past history was any indication, the chance for the survival of the few remaining Indians looked increasingly bleak.

But to read *Como era gostoso o meu francês* exclusively as an allegory about the demise of indigenous groups in the Northeast is to overlook its subtle implications for another kind of cultural imperialism that had begun in the mid-1950s, when President Juscelino Kubitschek opened the nation's doors to massive foreign investment in an attempt to rapidly transform Brazil into a modern industrial nation. That policy, known as "developmentalism," was ushered in during a democratic government and it included the building of Brasília and an influx of foreign capital from multinational corporations. After the 1968 coup, the country became increasingly dependent on foreign capital; despite continued high growth rates, the national debt burgeoned and disparities in income increased. The regime defended its policies and continued to use repressive measures to silence its detractors. But by the early seventies, the failure of the plan was becoming more evident; indeed, the much-touted economic "miracle" turned out to be a disaster, resulting in skyrocketing inflation, unemployment, increasing disparities in the distribution of income, and general social and political unrest.[13] The situation was akin to the colonial period: once the local resources were exhausted or no longer profitable, foreign companies moved on. In the meantime, the presence of those companies had already wrought vast changes in the culture. Since Brazil's independence, France had been a powerful cultural and intellectual force, but with developmentalism, the United States assumed unquestionable prominence. American television programs and music—not to mention the ever-popular Hollywood cinema—became increasingly cultural staples, and English replaced French as the most desirable foreign language to learn in schools and universities.

In the early twenties, Oswald de Andrade's "Manifesto Antropófago" had espoused the "ingestion" and adaptation of foreign ideas, which would supposedly function dialectically with the folkloric and popular cultures associated with Indians, thus creating a distinctive national identity. Nearly a half century later, *Como era gostoso o meu francês* takes up the same cannibalist theme; dos Santos's film, however, is suspicious of European influences and radically different in tone from Andrade's cannibalist manifesto, which had summarized its aims with the famous statement, "Tupy or not Tupy, that is the question." Unlike the "anthropophagous" movement (and unlike Joaquim Pedro de Andrade's 1969 film, *Macunaíma,* a wildly irreverent movie based on Mário de Andrade's 1928 fantastic novel about cannibalism and Brazilian culture), *Como era gostoso o meu francês* offers a subdued, unromantic portrait of a community that avenges any attack on its sovereignty by killing and devouring the invader. The Tupinambá in the film are neither the noble-savage heroes of the nineteenth-century European imagination nor the fierce mythopoetic symbols of twenties literary nationalism. They are, however, representatives of the postcolonial nation. What is most compelling about dos Santos's use of this familiar symbolism is his blending of "otherness" and "ordinariness" in the depiction of the Indians, who live a rather docile, mundane existence while trying to cope with foreign armies.

Dos Santos is not unrealistic about the ability of less technologically advanced countries like Brazil to keep foreign interests at bay; even so, he suggests by analogy or allegory that the contemporary culture is at risk. Like the Tupinambá, the current Brazilian citizens must be united in their desire to preserve their identity. The ritual of cannibalism becomes a metaphor for a paradoxical kind of modern consumerism that regards whatever is "devoured" as an alien substance and is careful to resist being utterly transformed by it. The consumption of any foreign element, the film seems to argue, ought to become a discriminating, proactive, even aggressive strategy; it should be highly selective about what it takes in, and it should ingest the foreign only to strengthen the local community.

In interviews given at the time the film was made, dos Santos underplayed the themes I have just described, insisting that *Como era gostoso o meu francês* was an "anthropological" as opposed to an "ideological" project. Perhaps he was being disingenuous, concealing his real purpose. And yet there can be no question of his efforts to faithfully replicate the lifestyle and language of a civilization that had suffered foreign invasion and extermination. He uses an approximation of Tupi (a lost language) for nearly all the dialogue, and he subtitles the film in Portuguese. (In this regard, he was being consistent with Staden, who describes everyone—including the French who pass through the Tupinambá village—as speaking Tupi.) In an even more daring move, he depicts the actual dress of the Indian community, which, according to Staden and others, consisted of little more than feathers, dye, and beads. (When casting, he even insisted that the actors have no surgical marks on their bodies.) Ironically, however, it was the ostensibly "anthropological" aspect of his film that ultimately caused problems with the Brazilian censors. The nakedness of the cast, especially of the white males, was strongly frowned upon by the government. Although the film was released abroad, it was initially suppressed nationwide because of its nudity; in fact, even the Cannes Film Festival committee rejected it on those grounds.[14]

It is important to note that the people in the film seem naked rather than nude. As John Berger and others have pointed out, "nudity" is a form of dress—a fetishized, artfully composed imagery of the human body that has a long history in European art. By contrast, dos Santos shows us people without clothes, and his practice is especially unorthodox when he allows us to see the frontal nakedness of Jean, who goes through most of the film wearing virtually nothing. Where Jean's particular nakedness is concerned, one of the common distinctions between literature and film as media becomes highly relevant. Because photography is not only iconic and symbolic but also indexical, dos Santos is able to provide us with a literal presentation of what Staden wrote about indirectly—and in so doing, he undermines the authority of the European. In Staden's work, we might say, we have the Phallus (a symbolic expression of European power and adventure controlled by a male voice), whereas in the film, we have the phallus (a body part, placed on view). This may explain why the Brazilian censors were more troubled by the naked Jean than by anything else in the film. In a wry essay, "De como evitar um homem nu" (How to Avoid a Naked Man), written for the *Jornal do Brasil,* the novelist Clarice Lispector, who had seen *Como era gostoso o meu francês* at a private showing and greatly admired it, takes issue with the government's decision to compromise on the unclothed Indians but not on the unclothed white captive. Responding to the censorship board's racism, which had been hidden under the guise of a kind of *National Geographic* conception of "anthropology," Lispector writes, "Perhaps it's my innocence, but kindly inform me: what is the difference between the naked body of an Indian male and the naked body of a white man?" (413).

With the appointment of a new head of the censorship bureau in November 1971, the film was finally granted exhibition rights throughout Brazil. Although dos Santos had characterized *Como era gostoso o meu francês* as an "anthropological" and not an "ideological" film, his particular use of historical texts and the images he juxtaposed with them clearly had a political purpose. We might say that he was attempting to reassess what Raymond Williams calls the "selective cultural tradition" by incorporating back into that tradition the lost record of the Tupinambá. As Williams points out, the historical record and the culture as a whole always involve a process of discrimination and omission:

> Within a given society, selection [of whatever is significant] will be governed by many kinds of special interests including class interests. Just as the actual social situation will largely govern *contemporary* selection, so the development of the society, the process of historical change, largely determine the selective tradition. The traditional culture of society will always tend to correspond to its contemporary system of interests and values, for it is not an absolute body of work but a continual selection and interpretation. (253)

Viewed in these terms, dos Santos's film is less interested in distorting a canonical text than in revealing what that text omits. Its documentary-like or "anthropological" style directly participates in an effort of reinterpretation by providing the viewer with a simulation of what has been lost, not just in time but also through the selective cultural process. Dos Santos's solidarity with the Tupinambá can therefore be described as an ideological position in powerful contrast with the interests and values of the dominant class in Brazil, which has always identified with Europeans, especially the French. His political statement, however, was indirect and was not completely apparent to everyone who first saw the film. In fact, despite his reassessment of the colonial encounter and the great attention and detail he gave to representing the Indians, the majority of the original audience in Brazil (including the censors) persisted in identifying with the French protagonist.[15] Dos Santos had nevertheless directed one of the most talked-about movies in the history of Brazilian cinema—a picture whose politics seem to become more clear with the passing years. After all, no matter what changes modernity has wrought, certain things have remained the same: Brazil's economy is still troubled and in one sense *Como era gostoso o meu francês*'s depiction of a rich local culture under siege is equally relevant for the colonial period, for the seventies, and for the present day.

An Experiment in Science Fiction: *Quem é Beta?*

Prior to the lifting of the ban on *Como era gostoso o meu francês* in Brazil, dos Santos was already working on a new project. After the success of *Como era gostoso o meu francês* at the Cannes Film Festival, the rights had been sold to the French, and dos Santos had met with the producer Gérard Léclery in Paris to discuss *Quem é Beta? (Pas de violence entre nous)* (Who Is Beta? [No Violence among Us]; 1973), a science fiction feature that would be his third and last movie made in the remote village of Parati.

Like his previous three features, *Quem é Beta?* is to some extent a work of countercinema that challenges the conventions of well-made narrative movies and shows the influence of Godard and the political avant-garde (in this case, as Johnson points out, there are some strong affinities with Godard's 1967 feature, *Weekend [Cinema* 199]). The story is at least nominally set in the future (the other side of the coin from a historical narrative such as *Como era gostoso o meu francês*), but it involves what Peter Wollen calls a "multiple diegesis" (499), allowing the time frame to shift unaccountably and anachronistic elements to appear. The characters have no psychological "depth" or development that would encourage the audience to feel identification or empathy. The plot, meanwhile, is open-ended and picaresque, with no indication of exactly when or where it takes place and often no clear motivation for the action. It begins in medias res as a young woman named Regina (Regina Rosemburgo), who is carrying a rifle and dressed in an outfit reminiscent of *One Million Years B.C.* (1966), walks along a highway strewn with car tires. As she makes her way along the road she comes across an abandoned truck; near it she shoots and kills a number of zombie-like people, known as "the contaminated," who cry out for food and water. (These figures bear a certain resemblance to the zombies in George Romero's 1967 horror film, *Night of the Living Dead.*) When she climbs to the summit of a hill, she becomes the target of a man named Maurício (Frédéric de Pasquale), who is gunning down the contaminated from a bunker-style house containing a machine gun, walkie-talkies, and sandbags. A siren on the house signals her approach, but Regina manages to convince Maurício that she is not an enemy. He takes her in and they proceed to defend the house from the contaminated. He also demonstrates the workings of an old movie camera that projects images of a way of life that no longer exists.

The film has a bizarre look that derives in part from the disjuncture between the futuristic-looking bunker and the prehistoric-style costumes. There are other disjunctures of this sort: Maurício's "video memory" camera is actually a relic from the silent era, a car that serves as a major prop is a 1928 Ford, and the characters' armaments consist of old-fashioned rifles and a machine gun from World War I. Dos Santos tells the amusing story that when his production chief went to the military to request some high-tech weapons to use in the film, he was arrested. Dos Santos was then summoned to military headquarters; after he explained to the minister of defense the purpose of his request, the official agreed to loan him a few Winchesters—a rifle that most Brazilian moviegoers would associate with films about turn-of-the-century Brazil and *cangaceiros* (Amancio 62). The use of these weapons was not a problem, however, because *Quem é Beta?* intentionally creates an apocalyptic world that is in some sense posthistorical or "out of time."

Soon after Regina and Maurício are established as a potential couple, a third character, a young woman named Beta (Sylvie Fennec), comes across the hilly terrain and into their lives (see fig. 10). After a brief stay, Beta decides to leave. "I'm tired of your memories," she says, and shortly thereafter Maurício goes in search of her. When he catches up to her, they make their way around the country, at one point visiting a sort of counterculture commune that grows vegetables and gives Tupi-like names to its leafy green products. One of the most bizarre sequences in the film occurs at this juncture. Maurício and Beta walk along the coast, accompanied by nondiegetic music that sounds like something from a holiday travelogue. Suddenly they begin to gun down the contaminated individuals who are quietly bathing in the water or walking along the shore. The scene is particularly unsettling because the couple laugh and playfully challenge one another, as if they were in a shooting gallery.

After a time Maurício decides to return to Regina, although his homecoming is less than welcoming; Regina and her new male companion, Gama (Dominque Rhule), shoot at him as he approaches the house. Once again, however, potential violent conflict dissolves into a companionable relationship. These three end up living together, occasionally

Figure 10. Sylvie Fen-
nec as Beta in *Quem
é Beta?* (Museum of
Modern Art/Film Stills
Archive)

donning gas masks and throwing gas bombs at one another as a form of
entertainment. During an approach of the contaminated, Beta reappears, amid siren wails, in an automobile. The characters rush forward
to meet her and another woman who is pregnant and resembles Beta.
Beta and this other woman appear interchangeably in a later scene in
which the five characters are sitting on the floor of the house having a
grand feast. As they gorge themselves on food, the contaminated clus-
ter around outside and stare at them through the windows. The film ends
suddenly as Gama and Regina, now in everyday modern dress, climb
aboard an Air France flight.

As Helena Salem points out, there is no "proper" way of reading

Quem é Beta? which has a loose narrative structure and a kind of dreamy, incoherent logic common to the drug culture of the seventies. There is, however, the possibility of understanding this film, like all of dos Santos's work, as a kind of allegorical commentary on the state of the nation. At the time the film was made, the economic miracle promoted by the military dictatorship as the salve to Brazil's ills was a clear failure. Brazilian society was even more divided into haves and have-nots, much like the film's two chief groups: those who have guns, food, and shelter, and those who wander about the landscape crying out for food and water. *Quem é Beta?* is not the first dos Santos film to describe the extremes of the class structure in Brazil, but it is certainly one of his most unusual and aggressive treatments of the subject in its depiction of warring classes and of the future of Brazilian modernity as a tropical wasteland.

Perhaps it was because the public had not understood *Azyllo muito louco* (or had understood it too well) that the distributors asked dos Santos to film a prologue to *Quem é Beta?* that would explicitly tell audiences not to look for any message in the film and not to believe in its dramatic "realism." In this prologue, dos Santos likens the film to a comic strip, and he tells viewers to get comfortable, relax, and simply enjoy the action. Even if dos Santos actually believed what he was saying, the prologue can only be read ironically. In fact, it prepares viewers for something unusual and experimental, something that can be enjoyed only as an allegory or as a kind of oneiric, dystopian vision.

If the actors in *Quem é Beta?* were unsure of the film's subject—and this appears to be the case, at least based on a comment by Arduíno Colasanti, who had a small part in the movie (Salem 275)—then it is not surprising that the public and critics were equally baffled. The local critical response was especially negative. "Only one film critic in the world liked the film," dos Santos has said, referring to Carlos Diegues, who defended the movie in a long article entitled "Who Is Better?" in the June 27, 1973, issue of the Rio newspaper *Última hora* (Last Hour). The critical reception in France was also negative. Dos Santos recalls showing the film to some friends at the Cannes Film Festival and their subsequent reaction: they took him out to lunch, told him to pretend that the picture never existed, and advised him to return to Brazil and make another movie that could compete at the festival (Amancio 64). And that is exactly what he did.

For a Popular Cinema: *O amuleto de Ogum,*
Tenda dos milagres, and *Estrada da vida*

Dos Santos once remarked that *Fome de amor, Azyllo muito louco,* and *Quem é Beta?* were products of his increasing alienation from Brazil: "'In truth, that whole period of metaphorical, investigative films turned into a road without end. By that I mean that it did not offer a solution, [ideas] were drying up, and there was nothing more to invent'" (qtd. in Amancio 65). By the time he returned to Brazil to begin work on *O amuleto de Ogum* in 1973, the reign of terror associated with the Medici government was coming to a close. In 1974, a new military administration came to power under the leadership of Ernesto Geisel, who initiated the transition toward a political *abertura* (opening) and a gradual return to a democratic form of government. Even though government repression was still in effect, Geisel's initiatives to change the political course of the country stimulated all sectors of society, particularly the arts. For dos Santos, the ability to make films without fear of government reprisals resulted in his return from cultural exile and a renewed commitment to a kind of Brazilian cinema that would appeal first and foremost to *o povo.* At the same time, Embrafilme, the major distributor of Brazilian films, was undergoing considerable restructuring, leading to the selection of the filmmaker Roberto Farias to head the agency.[16] As a result of the joint efforts of Farias and filmmakers such as dos Santos, who participated in discussions about how the agency could best serve its constituencies, Embrafilme became more flexible in its policies and more supportive of local directors.

Dos Santos's new coproduced project with Embrafilme, *O amuleto de Ogum,* was based on an earlier script, *O amuleto da morte* (The Amulet of Death) by Francisco Santos about the rise of Caxias, a city in the state of Rio that was becoming a major settlement for northeastern migrants. Dos Santos rewrote the script, adding a crime story about a politically powerful racketeer in Caxias as well as several scenes about umbanda—a popular religion, practiced for the most part secretly, whose origins hark back to the colonial period. The result is a film that blends the crime genre, one that dos Santos had worked with before in *Boca de Ouro,* with a spectacular but suppressed aspect of Brazilian popular culture.

O amuleto de Ogum is structured as a story within a story. Firmino (Jards Macalé), a blind man who plays a guitar and sings story-ballads to earn a modest living, is beaten and robbed by three hoodlums in an alleyway in Caxias. After robbing Firmino, the hoodlums demand that he perform for them. One of them wants to hear the story of Pedro Álvares Cabral, the Portuguese navigator credited as the first European to reach Brazil in 1500; another wants to hear a story based on Bocage, a character in pornographic jokes told in both Portugal and Brazil. Firmino ignores their requests and informs them that he will tell them a true story. He begins the tale with the title "O amuleto de Ogum."

The protagonist of Firmino's story and of the ensuing film is a young northeasterner named Gabriel whose father and brother are killed while working in the fields near their home in Palmeiras. Gabriel's mother (Maria Ribeiro), fearful of losing her only surviving child to an assassin's bullet, takes him to a *pai-de-santo* (priest) to seek the protection of the umbanda divinities. A ceremony is performed to give divine protection to Gabriel, who lies on a table covered with various religious artifacts (see fig. 11). At the conclusion of the ceremony, a necklace is hung around his neck. The importance of the necklace is suggested as the camera slowly pans down the boy's torso to a point close to his waist, where an amulet hangs at the end of a chain.

The next scene takes place ten years later, when an older Gabriel (played by dos Santos's son, Ney Sant'Anna) gets off a bus in Caxias. He carries with him a letter from Clóvis, a friend of his family who has sent Gabriel to live with his *compadre*, Severiano (Jofre Soares), a prominent townsman and local racketeer. In the letter, Clóvis informs Severiano that Gabriel has a magical *corpo fechado* (closed body) and that he is immune to physical injury and even death. Severiano is amused by what he regards as his old friend's superstitious beliefs; nonetheless, he makes Gabriel part of his household entourage of gunmen and killers. A short time later, Severiano is made aware of the truth of Clóvis's statement. Chico (Francisco Santos), one of Severiano's henchmen, shoots Gabriel at the dinner table as a result of an argument precipitated by a bungled assassination. When the bullets fail to penetrate Gabriel's body, Chico and the other gunmen approach him as if he were a divinity and celebrate his invincibility. As Gabriel is carried off on the shoulders of his comrades, the camera slowly pans up a long staircase to a landing,

Figure 11. Preparing the *corpo fechado* with
Maria Ribeiro as Gabriel's mother looking on in
O amuleto de Ogum. (Museum of Modern Art/
Film Stills Archive)

where a large statue of St. George sits. The camera movement emphasizes the statue's significance, drawing our attention to the quasi-deity whose traditional role was to protect warriors.

The next part of the film concerns the growing tensions between Severiano and Gabriel that result from an attraction between Severiano's young wife, Eneida (Anecy Rocha), and Gabriel. After unknowingly assassinating the popular president of the local Red Cross at Severiano's instruction, Gabriel is forced to hide out. Although someone else is ultimately framed for the murder, Gabriel forms his own gang of mostly neighborhood youngsters whose criminal activities threaten Severiano's gambling operations. Severiano seeks Gabriel's downfall and begins killing off his band one by one; he also orders two of his henchmen to visit a less than reputable *pai-de-santo* (Washington Fernandes), who extracts payment for his attempts to open up Gabriel's *corpo fechado*. Although unsuccessful, the priest does weaken Gabriel through rituals that compel him to drink alcohol. One evening, the gunmen overpower a drunken Gabriel, who has passed out in a motel room; they wrap him up in a canvas tarp and shoot bullets into his body before dumping him into the sea. The respected umbanda leader Pai Erley (an actual *pai-de-santo* who plays himself) and his followers pull the tarp out of the water after the gunmen leave. When they open the canvas, they find Gabriel with his eyes wide open, a smile on his face, and his hand wrapped tightly around the amulet.

When Severiano learns of Gabriel's magical escape from death, he contacts Eneida, who agrees to seduce Gabriel and remove his amulet in exchange for money. This plot also fails, so Severiano, believing that Gabriel's mother's death will end Gabriel's divine protection, orders two of his henchmen to kill her. The gunmen bungle the job by shooting her cleaning lady who resembles the mother, but Severiano sends out word of the mother's death. Pai Erley, with whom Gabriel is staying and from whom he is receiving instruction in umbanda, passes on the tragic news. A distraught Gabriel seeks out Severiano and a gun battle ensues. The shoot-out is treated in a stylized, fantastic form, with Severiano appearing and disappearing before Gabriel's eyes as if he were the Devil. Severiano ultimately succeeds in shooting Gabriel in the back. Apparently mortally wounded, Gabriel kills Severiano before falling into a swimming pool. Face down in the water, his body slowly begins to move; we cut to a shot of his mother, who fears for her son's life after the earlier attempt on her own as she steps off a bus in Caxias. In the final scene, Gabriel's body is magically transported from the swimming pool to the sea, where he leaps out of the water and onto a boat, two pistols raised in his hands—as if he were the incarnation of the warrior-god (see fig. 12). The film now comes full circle by returning to the scene with Firmino and the hoodlums, who are unhappy with the blind man's story. They decide to kill him, but their weapons prove useless; it turns out that, like the protagonist of his true but miraculous tale, Firmino has a *corpo fechado*. Impervious to their bullets and knife thrusts, he pulls out a large knife and kills all three attackers. As he walks away, he sings a song with the refrain: "I go, I kill, I die / and I return to enjoy."

O amuleto de Ogum brings together themes and characters that hark back to dos Santos's earliest films. As Johnson notes, dos Santos's casting is directly linked to *Vidas secas*: Maria Ribeiro, who played Sinhá Vitória

Figure 12. Ney Sant'Anna as the older Gabriel in
O amuleto de Ogum. (Museum of Modern Art/
Film Stills Archive)

in the earlier film, is the mother in *O amuleto de Ogum* and the scene in
which she and the young Gabriel cross the desert-like northeastern terrain to reach the umbanda temple is reminiscent of the introduction to
Vidas secas in which Sinhá Vitória and her family struggle across the *sertão*
(*Cinema* 202). Jofre Soares, who played the intemperate landowner in
Vidas secas, returns to play an even less sympathetic role as Severiano.
There is still another, more subtle connection between the two films. In
one of *O amuleto de Ogum*'s most memorable scenes, Severiano's henchmen torture a young boy who works for Gabriel in an attempt to find out
where the rest of his gang is hiding. The boy is strung up by his arms and
legs and rotated on a metal fixture that looks like an old-fashioned clothes-
line. On the soundtrack, we hear a grating noise produced by the metal
pole as it swings the boy around. The sound is composed of the same sin-
gularly distinct, dissonant noise of the squeaking oxcart wheel that has
become synonymous with the poor and desperate lives in *Vidas secas.*

Johnson quite rightly suggests that *O amuleto de Ogum* might be looked upon as a sequel to *Vidas secas* in that it focuses on what happens to the northeasterner who reaches the large city (*Cinema* 202). He also calls attention to how in *O amuleto de Ogum* dos Santos returns to the urban setting of his first two films, *Rio, 40 graus* and *Rio, Zona Norte* (*Cinema* 202). There are also marked differences from the earlier work. The *favela* of the fifties portrayed in dos Santos's first two films appears almost pastoral in comparison to seventies Caxias, where robbery and murder are commonplace and where a northeasterner like Gabriel, who has left one violent land for another, becomes a strong and volatile presence.

But what most distinguishes *O amuleto de Ogum* from dos Santos's earlier work, including the crime film *Boca de Ouro,* is the emphasis it gives to the popular culture of the Northeast, where elements of magic and myth commingle with activities of everyday life. For example, at one point Mr. Baraúna (Emmanuel Cavalcanti), Severiano's lawyer, muses about the plot to murder Gabriel, noting that it is similar to the killing of Lampião, a legendary northeastern bandit. This statement is vigorously challenged by Quati, one of Severiano's men from the Northeast, who regards the lawyer's comment as a personal affront: "Lampião didn't die sleeping. Lampião died fighting on his feet! Lampião wasn't a man to die sleeping, Mr. Baraúna. Come now, a man of your intelligence saying something stupid like that!" A broader, more sympathetic commentary on northeastern attitudes and mores is presented in a scene toward the end of the film, when Eneida takes Gabriel for a brief visit to her family's home in São Paulo. Unlike life in Caxias, which is associated with political alliances, cronyism, and cut-throat gangs, here the northeastern family unit has remained intact, and hard-working individuals are closely bound to one another. Eneida's homecoming causes her parents, both migrants from the Northeast, and the rest of her family to rejoice; they celebrate by preparing a special meal of *sarapatel* (a dish made with blood, kidneys, lungs, and hearts of sheep with broth), which is served with *cachaça,* a strong alcoholic drink made from sugar cane. The scene ends with the family members dancing to *forró* music played by a trio of northeasterners—a decided contrast with the contemporary music and sinister atmosphere of the Boate Moustache in Caxias, a bar that doubles as a night club and brothel, where criminals hang out.

Another important difference between *O amuleto de Ogum* and dos Santos's first two films can be seen in the way the later picture integrates religion into the overall view of contemporary society. There are no references to candomblé, macumba, or umbanda in *Rio, 40 graus* or *Rio, Zona Norte*, even though both films take a supposedly realistic approach to life in the *favela*, where such religions are practiced on a broad scale. The emphasis on religion in *O amuleto de Ogum* can be partly explained by how strong an impact Jorge Amado's novel *Tenda dos milagres* (Tent of Miracles; 1972), about African-Brazilian culture and religion, had on dos Santos as he was working on the film and how it led him to appreciate the significance of religion to the poor. Dos Santos also attributes his changed attitude to his wife, Laurita, who was taking an anthropology course at the time and who shared with him ideas about society, religion, and culture. In addition, he benefited from the knowledge and contacts of his long-time friend Erley José Freitas, an umbandista whom dos Santos had known since making *Rio, Zona Norte*. Not surprisingly, dos Santos chose him to play Pai Erley, the "good" *pai-de-santo* who pulls Gabriel from the sea, gives him instruction in umbanda, and deftly rebuffs Severiano.

Although dos Santos had long been aware of religious practices in the *favela*, his approach in his earliest films was strictly Marxist, focusing on social class and race while implicitly dismissing religion as an opiate of the masses. *O amuleto de Ogum* makes clear not only the centrality of religion in the lives of the poor but also the ways in which umbanda reinforces class solidarity and gives a kind of power to individuals who are caught in a violent and corrupt world. As dos Santos notes in a 1975 interview:

> When I made *Rio, 40 Graus,* I spent nearly a year walking through the *favela*, visiting the group of young boys, going to macumba sessions, and running into the religious practice of messages or dispatches. But my camera wasn't filming any of this. I totally ignored the religious view of the people as well as their own view of the world. The reality that I sought wasn't before the camera but rather in the model that I held in my head. And that is what happened to Brazilian cinema.
>
> The point of departure for the film [*O amuleto de ogum*] was uncovering the popular view of our reality and trying to take it into the movie theaters, certain that a popular film would be commercially successful,

thereby resolving the financial situation. Statistics show that 60 million Brazilians do not go to the movies because the cinema has nothing to do with them. It's a new and open market. (Beraba 3)

It is important to note that at the time the movie was made, umbanda, candomblé, and macumba temples were strictly forbidden by the military regime unless they were formally registered (along with brothels and other similar venues)—a clear indication of the government's uneasiness with popular assemblage. As a result, people practiced their religion clandestinely. Given the government's hard line against umbanda, dos Santos took a particularly bold step when he decided to represent its strong community presence as well as its beliefs and practices. Stam writes that "the film simply assumes *umbandista* values, without explaining them to the uninitiated" (267); and he points out that "the film does not idealize *umbanda:* one *umbanda* priest in the film works for popular liberation; the other is a greedy charlatan and opportunist" (268). *O amuleto de Ogum* was equally daring in its realistic portrayal of torture, which had been practiced regularly by the military regime. The government censors, however, seemed not to understand the broader implications of the film. According to dos Santos, they demanded that only one of the more graphic scenes of torture be cut and the picture was released without difficulty in 1975.

Despite dos Santos's desire to make a movie that would have strong popular appeal, *O amuleto de Ogum* was not commercially successful; it ended up being marketed as an art film and was restricted to small theaters.[17] A special showing was arranged in Caxias, where it was well received by the local community. It also received favorable critical notices and was selected to compete at the Cannes Film Festival as well as at the Gramado Film Festival, where it won the prize for best picture. In looking back at the film, dos Santos appears to have been pleased with it. At one point he remarked on the symbolic significance of the framing story, observing that the singer who refuses to comply with requests to recycle familiar material and who opts to tell his own tale is analogous to the best directors of Brazilian cinema, who have their own "corpo fechado" (Amancio 218). Although *O amuleto de Ogum* did not gain the kind of public reception that dos Santos had hoped for, he did not change course. His commitment to the idea of a popular cinema and to the representation of African-Brazilian religion was so strong that when he learned of the businessman Ronald Levinson's interest in producing a movie, he immediately proposed an adaptation of Amado's *Tenda dos milagres.*

Like the novel on which it is based, the film *Tenda dos milagres* focuses on the world of high society, academia, and big business in Salvador, Bahia—a city that has the largest black population in Brazil. The same elements of political power, greed, and violence that make up the underworld of Caxias in *O amuleto de Ogum* are also at the heart of this film. The basic difference between the two is that instead of resorting to torture and killings, the power elite in *Tenda dos milagres* employ less obvious and less violent means to defend and promote their status and wealth. These include the social registers, local histories, institutional policies, and laws they author, plus the power and persuasion of the media, which they either own or with which they are allied. (In Althusserian terms, the first film might be said to deal with a repressive apparatus, whereas the second deals with an ideological apparatus.) As in *O amuleto de Ogum,* popular religion plays a central role in *Tenda dos milagres,* becoming one of the means by which a disadvantaged group counters a decadent and oppressive establishment, creating a sense of community and solidarity for the city's largely poor and black population.

The structure of the two films is also similar in the sense that both rely upon a framing device. In *O amuleto de Ogum,* as we have seen, the story is told by the blind singer, Firmino, who appears not only at the beginning and the end of the film but also at certain junctures during the narrative, as if to comment on the "truth" that lies behind his tale. In *Tenda dos milagres,* the framing device is provided by a down-at-the-heels writer and filmmaker, Fausto Pena (Hugo Carvana), who is making a movie about the life of the mulatto Pedro Arcanjo, an amateur philosopher and sociologist who worked as a beadle in the local university at the beginning of the twentieth century. Although he died in relative obscurity in the forties, Arcanjo has been suddenly cast into the public spotlight as a result of the attention and praise given to his work on African culture and religion by an American anthropologist and Nobel Prize winner, Dr. James D. Livingstone (Laurence R. Wilson), who has come to Salvador to learn more about Arcanjo.[18]

The framing story of the search to find out more about Pedro Arcanjo, together with Fausto Pena's desire to capitalize on Arcanjo's celebrity by making a movie about him, frequently interrupt the main narrative, which consists of a chronology of events in the life of Arcanjo—events that Pena has researched and that we see him editing at the beginning of the film. As both Johnson and Salem have pointed out, the framing device is even more complex as a result of a brief pre-credits appearance of a television weather broadcast that informs the viewer: "In Bahia, the weather is good" (Johnson, *Cinema* 206; Salem 310). Although there is no return to the television at the end of the film, its initial appearance suggests a (partial) frame for a movie which, in turn, is constructed around the idea of a film within a film. Here and elsewhere, dos Santos calls attention to the presence and power of media in everyday life and to the mediated quality of all modern experience, even when it is narrated to us in a quasi-folkloric form. As he states in an interview with Johnson, "In reality, [*Tenda dos milagres*] is a television spectacle, as if you arrived home, turned on the set and watched what happened" ("Interview" 14).

O amuleto de Ogum and *Tenda dos milagres* share other traits. For example, both Gabriel and Arcanjo (whose name translates as "archangel") have names that evoke the biblical. Gabriel's *corpo fechado* enables him to escape harm and ultimately transforms him into a pistol-waving warrior-protector; Arcanjo has the "eyes of Xangô," which is a translation of "Ojuabá," the name he is known by in the black community. As Ojuabá, the most powerful deity in candomblé, he affirms his beliefs in the African gods and rituals and defends his people from harm. In one of the film's most dramatic scenes, Arcanjo uses his powers to transform Zé da Grande Alma (Big Soul Joe), a candomblé-believer-turned-police-henchman, into a wrathful avenger of the black community who attacks the police chief and refuses to obey the command that he kill a candomblé priest.

The major difference between the two movies is the larger presence that candomblé has in *Tenda dos milages* as compared to the more elliptical and fragmented presentation of umbanda in *O amuleto de Ogum*. *Tenda dos milagres* paints a broader picture of religion, focusing on the place of worship, the congregation, the rituals, and particularly the music, which is a crucial element in the ceremonies. *Tenda dos milagres* is also a more ironic and satiric movie than *O amuleto de Ogum*. For example, it pokes fun at a certain kind of Brazilianist academic—a figure who is wonderfully lampooned in the aptly named Dr. Livingstone, who arrives in Salvador from the United States and creates a local media frenzy by praising the long-forgotten Arcanjo and his theories about miscegenation and democracy. The athletic-looking Livingstone, a Nobel laureate who sports the traditional academic beard and pipe, is especially interested in having sex with Ana Mercedes (Sonia Dias), a mulatta whom he meets at the press conference and publicly declares is "the greatest living example" of Arcanjo's theories. Ana accepts money from Livingstone in return for sex but makes an outspoken critique of him, remarking that he has photographed her in the nude as if she were a wild animal. This segment of the film also serves as an implicit critique of the sex industry in Brazil, especially in the Northeast, which is designed to appeal to certain foreigners. Even today, special travel packages designed for Europeans and Americans include arrangements to have sex with dark-skinned young women whose images are fundamental to the industry's marketing strategy.

By changing the novel's Fausto Pena character from a scholar-narrator to a poet-moviemaker, dos Santos also adds a tongue-in-cheek commentary on the Brazilian film industry. Throughout his work on the film-within-the-film, Pena is repeatedly frustrated in his attempts to make an appointment with Embrafilme's Roberto Farias (the actual head of the agency at the time), with whom he wants to talk about funding his movie. Not only does the film satirize Embrafilme's inaccessibility but it also questions its values. Hanging on the wall behind the table where Pena makes his calls to the agency is a large poster publicizing a pornographic film entitled *Amadas e violentadas* (Loved and Violated). The scene is both comical and darkly ironic, indirectly commenting on the contradictory nature of Embrafilme, especially prior to its 1975 reformulation. (Under the administration of the ultraconservative military government, the agency gave generous funding to *pornochanchadas* and other sexually explicit movies at the same time that it refused to fund serious, socially committed films by directors associated with the Cinema Novo.) Ultimately, Fausto Pena abandons all hope of securing funding. (His name connotes both his financial pact with the "devil" Livingstone, for whom he researches for payment the life of Arcanjo, and the shame and pain [*pena*] caused by Livingstone's sexual fling with Ana, who is his girlfriend.) Dos Santos gets in a final lick at Embrafilme in the last conversation between Fausto and Ana. Having had his consciousness raised by his research on Arcanjo, Fausto informs her that he no longer cares about finishing the movie—and with a sly chuckle he says that the audience has just seen it anyway.

Various American critics, including Joan Dessin, Marsha Kinder, Johnson, and Stam, have written extensive and favorable commentaries on this film. Dessin, however, is less enthusiastic about the narrative shifts between past and present in the film, which she describes as clumsy (37–38). I find the alternation between the two time frames simply unexpected and abrupt. *Tenda dos milagres* challenges its viewers to make the sort of connections that most Hollywood films present smoothly. The narrative comes off as somewhat disorienting primarily because two different actors play the role of Pedro Arcanjo at different stages of his life. Far from a Buñuelian device, this was the result of Jards Macalé's decision to leave the project in the middle of filming. Since dos Santos could not afford to reshoot the scenes with Macalé's substitute, Juarez Paraíso, he decided to keep the original footage with Macalé, who plays the youthful Arcanjo, and to cast Paraíso as the mature Arcanjo (see fig. 13). Despite a solid performance by Paraíso, who had no professional acting experience, his sudden appearance in the film, without any mention of the passage of time or the usual preparations to allow the suspension of disbelief, has an estranging effect. Dos Santos tries to ameliorate the problem at the beginning of the film, when a reference to Arcanjo is accompanied by a brief glimpse of both actors. But this occurs too early in the movie and is too elliptical a reference for most viewers to grasp its significance.

Chiefly by virtue of its framing device, *Tenda dos milagres* is highly self-reflexive; indeed, the ideological implications of telling a story (or of making a movie) are as central to its concerns as the narrative about Arcanjo and turn-of-the-century Bahia. Although the central plot, replete with religious and ideological battles waged between Arcanjo and his archenemy, the medical school professor and white supremacist Nilo Argolo (Nildo Parente), is fascinating to watch, the film uses various techniques—including shifting time frames, the abrupt change in actors, winks and nods about the film industry, and tongue-in-cheek character-

Figure 13. Juarez Paraíso as the older Pedro Arcanjo in *Tenda dos milagres.* (Nelson Pereira dos Santos collection)

izations—to keep audience members aware that they are watching mediated events. Its tone throughout is playfully satiric, with broadly drawn characters such as Argolo and Livingstone; the greedy advertising executives of Doping, Inc., who capitalize off the Arcanjo media frenzy by naming a shopping center after him and marketing a new deodorant called Fresh Black; and the upstanding and "liberally minded" Colonel Gomes (Jofre Soares), who regards his son's best friend from the university, Tadeu Canhoto (a mulatto, who is also Arcanjo's son), "as if he were his own son," at least until Tadeu threatens to become an actual part of his family by asking the colonel for his daughter's hand in marriage. Soares, in the role of Gomes, adds to this effect by giving another of his outstanding performances as a disreputable type; his refined manners in the early part of the movie give way to outrageous fits of shouting and arm-waving when he learns his family's lineage might be tainted with Tadeu's black blood. His racism is equally evident when he visits a newly appointed police chief to complain about his family situation. Unlike the former police chief, who was dismissed for his role in the bungled assassination of a candomblé priest, the new official offers no salves to Gomes and even proudly announces that he himself is a mulatto. Shocked that a mulatto would be placed in such a high office, Gomes rants at the even-tempered police chief, calling him "Dr. Mestiço" (Dr. Mixed-Blood) over his shoulder as he stomps out of his office.

Despite Argolo's claims of a "racially pure" background and despite vigorous protestations against miscegenation, many characters are shown to be of mixed blood, and it is suggested that virtually everyone, including those from the highest levels of Bahian society, has at least one African ancestor. (The early credit sequence, which creates a collage of various sepia-tinted, turn-of-the-century photographs of light-skinned society gentlemen in formal attire alongside rich, colorful images of African Brazilians, clearly anticipates this point.) Argolo is totally undone by Arcanjo's research into the African heritage of the elite, which is published by a printer friend in a shop called Tenda dos Milagres. Arcanjo gets special satisfaction by dedicating the book to "his cousin Nilo Argolo," with whom he discovers, to his surprise and delight, that he shares a black ancestor. Unfortunately, however, Arcanjo loses his job at the university and is arrested and jailed for his writings. After his release, we see him taking up the Allied cause against Hitler, and he dies at a table in a house of prostitution after participating in an anti-Nazi street demonstration.

The film ends on an ironic note as it shifts to the present-day: As a result of his newfound celebrity, Arcanjo is granted a posthumous degree by the same university where he worked as a beadle and was attacked for his writings on African-Brazilian cultural identity. With great pomp and circumstance, his portrait is hung on the wall and he is transformed into a kind of sentimental icon for a consumer-oriented culture. The final scene and the post-credits offer a different reading of the past: As a parade commemorating a nineteenth-century Bahian movement to liberate Brazil from imperial rule passes along the street, the camera follows a group of celebrating black Bahians. The words "Independência ou Morte" (Independence or Death) appear prominently on the screen—a rallying cry for a black population that now fills the entire frame.

A primary complaint made by Brazilian and U.S. critics against Amado's novel was about its implicit argument for miscegenation as the way to achieve true democracy. Stam observes that this idea is presented in the novel without any discussion or even hint of the problematic "whitening process" for a mostly black population that underlies race mixing (see 299–307). Nor is there any critique in Amado's work of a society that prefers to be called white when it is predominantly black (a 2001 poll conducted in Brazil shows that only 5 percent of the people identified themselves as black [Jones 15]). Another criticism has been aimed at Amado's characterizations of the hypersexuality supposedly found in blacks and in the African religion. The book introduces Arcanjo by describing his adventures with various women and strongly emphasizing his sexual prowess. Dos Santos was probably aware of both problems when filming, although he does not alter or critique the argument for race mixing. Instead, he omits most of Arcanjo's sexual encounters and tries to avoid stereotyping him. The film's only graphic sex scene involves Arcanjo and Kirsi (Liana Maria Graff), a Norwegian. Their relationship, as Stam points out, implicitly suggests an unproblematic "'progression' from Arcanjo, the mulatto, to his child by a white Scandinavian woman" (306); the relationship is also presented in a romantic way, without any of the titillation we find in the book. In fact, the film focuses on a man of integrity, intelligence, and religious belief who struggles his entire life against racism and political oppression. In this sense, the movie offers a more sensitive and positive view of black Bahian society, including the religion of candomblé, which is treated artfully, respectfully, and without any of the stereotypical sexual references that all too often have diminished Amado's novels about the African-Brazilian community.

Dos Santos followed up his critically acclaimed *Tenda dos milagres* with *Estrada da vida (Milionário e José Rico)* (The Road of Life [Milionário and José Rico]; 1981), a rags-to-prosperity story about the misadventures of a pair of country singers, Milionário and José Rico, who are famous in Brazil and who play themselves in the movie. According to José Mário Ortiz Ramos, more than a million Brazilians saw this picture in its first year of release—an amazing success in what was a particularly dismal year for the Brazilian film industry (444). But unlike the general public, who were entertained by *Estrada da vida*'s straightforward humor and musical numbers, the critics were nearly unanimous in their disdain. They were especially displeased with what they regarded as the movie's benign portrait of capitalism and the music industry, and they criticized dos Santos for having made a commercial project to promote Milionário and José Rico's record sales. As Salem notes, had it not been for the box office success of *Estrada da vida,* the situation would have been a repeat of the disastrous release of *Quem é Beta?* Years later, dos Santos recalled the barrage of critical attacks against *Estrada da vida,* saying that it was "'horrible, like nothing you can imagine'" (qtd. in Salem 325).

Estrada da vida, however, is far from being a defense of capitalism or simply a promotional vehicle for the *sertaneja dupla* (country singer duo). There is no question that Milionário and José Rico's popularity, already well established in Brazil when the film was made, was bolstered by the movie and that their record sales increased locally as well as internationally—even in places as unlikely as China, where they were invited to perform. Yet *Estrada da vida* is also an affectionate and vivid film about the migration of poor and dispossessed Brazilians from the countryside to the big city. In this regard, it offers a unique and positive view of everyday life among the urban working poor—a utopian sense of energy, sincerity, and community that has rarely been portrayed in Brazilian cinema.

The film is particularly interesting to contemplate in light of the important issues raised by Richard Dyer in his well-known essay "Entertainment and Utopia," which is chiefly concerned with classical Hollywood musicals. As Dyer points out, the appeal of such movies lies in their addressing of real and not simply imaginary needs. Hollywood pictures about song, dance, and "show biz" are fundamentally utopian in form, even if they are not politically progressive. In response to scarcity or poverty, they give us an image of abundance and shared prosperity; in response to alienated labor and the dreariness of urban life, they provide the energy and intensity of musical performance; in response to the manipulation of advertising and the duplicity of social relations, they depict open, spontaneous, and honest characters; and in response to the fragmentation of modern life, they offer a world of community and collective activity. The problem, of course, is that the gap between the real world and the world on the screen, and the attendant social contradictions this gap threatens to reveal, is usually papered over or bought off by nostalgia (as in 1944's *Meet Me in St. Louis* or 2001's *Moulin Rouge*), primitivism (as in all-black musicals like *Cabin in the Sky* [1943] or *Porgy and Bess* [1959]), or by the dubious idea that capitalist entertainment can solve all the problems that capitalism itself creates (as in show biz musicals like *Forty-Second Street* [1933] or *The Band Wagon* [1953]). Ultimately, as Dyer explains, Hollywood gives us "what utopia would feel like rather than how it would be organized" (177).

We cannot live without utopian impulses or the desire for a better world, because such things make social progress possible. But there are different kinds of artistic utopias. Dos Santos's film about music and show biz is a case in point. It makes an intriguing contrast to the Hollywood musical, and also to the Brazilian *chanchada,* which usually operates along similar lines. Like most musicals, *Estrada da vida* gives us a sense of utopian energy and community, but at the same time it shows scarcity, inequality, alienated labor, and duplicity of everyday life under capitalism. It makes no political speeches and is always light-hearted and comic, but it represents poor and working-class people quite realistically, paying tribute to their utopian forms of entertainment and to the solidarity their entertainment nourishes.

It should be noted that *Estrada da vida* was made during the years associated with the political *abertura* in Brazil as well as in the spirit of the Federation of Cineclubs' 1975 publication, "Manifesto por um cinema popular," in which dos Santos discusses the need for a cinema that will focus on the people, appeal to a large audience, and compete at the box office with U.S. and other foreign imports. In dos Santos's words: "The people will recognize themselves in a film that not only bases itself on popular values but also accepts and projects them positively. As a consequence, as the people affirm themselves culturally by going to the movies, they also give economic support to the production" (6–7). In his essay entitled "O amuleto mudou tudo" (The Amulet Changed Everything) that also appears in this publication, Jean-Claude Bernardet elaborates on dos Santos's notion of what a popular cinema should be:

> The audience is no longer regarded as a mass of people to be seduced in some way so that they buy tickets at the box office, but rather as a segment of society for whom the production and exhibition of the film signifies a social identification, a recognition of themselves, their being, their values, their potentialities and their limitations. . . . The spectacle shown by the film is no longer of a form of oppression from top to bottom, or of the entertainment industry oppressing the public, but rather an attempt at a dramatic representation that is born at the bottom and moves to the top. (11)

Dos Santos's change in course from orthodox Marxism to left-wing populism can be traced back to *O amuleto de Ogum* and *Tenda dos milagres,* which treat in a sympathetic way the religious practices of umbanda and candomblé, showing their importance in the lives of poor and working-class Brazilians. A scene in *Tenda dos milagres,* in which the beleaguered but unbowed hero of the film, Pedro Arcanjo, rejects the Marxist discourse of a university professor, is significant in this regard. As a mulatto staff assistant in a predominantly white, upper-middle-class university population, Arcanjo prefers the solidarity that he derives from candomblé over the friendly professor's well-intentioned yet abstract argument about world revolution and class struggle. In an interview with Johnson, dos Santos comments on the professor:

> [The professor] represents the orthodox Marxist who throughout the years has been just as colonizing as the non-Marxist colonizer because he has not been able to transfer the mode of thought but has instead merely transferred the observations achieved through that method. . . . I am criticizing myself as well, because I have fallen into the same trap. It's part of my being—this attitude that we call sociological, distanced, elitist, professorial, removed from the reality of the people and their interests. An intellectual like the professor . . . envisions the transformation of society. He is sincere about this, but his life of social mobility— first he becomes a professor, then director of the institute—is a contradiction. His background, his class, and position prevent him from including truly popular manifestations—specifically religion—in his cultural universe. ("Toward" 139)

In an interview with the *Jornal do Brasil,* which appeared shortly after making *Estrada da vida,* dos Santos states his position unequivocally in the face of his detractors: "'I avoided the authoritarian discourse of the director who has the power to impose on the viewer a reductionist and all-too-well-known sociological view. . . . The language of cinema is emotion. Enough with sociology in film. It can be useful to draw from in the preparation of a film, and later for whomever wishes to utilize it in order to talk about the movie. But sociology in the mouths of the characters—never'" (qtd. in Salem 324–26). Although critics were shocked by dos Santos's pronouncement, which seemed to conflict with his Marxist beliefs, they should have recalled the position that he set forth in 1975: "A person never stops participating politically when they participate culturally. The intention is not to abandon a political vision, but rather to have that political vision within the cultural practice" ("Manifesto" 10).

Although *Estrada da vida* is more fanciful and gently amusing than anything dos Santos had done previously, it also makes its political point by taking as its subject a style of music that at the time was ignored, if not disdained, by middle- and upper-class audiences. Dos Santos continues, as in earlier films, to explore the culture of a marginalized segment of the Brazilian population; but here he seems to feel, or at least to encourage, a far greater identification with the people who are being filmed: "The reality I was looking for [in films such as *Rio, 40 graus*] wasn't what was in front of the cameras but rather was in the model that I had in my head" ("Manifesto" 4). His decision to make *Estrada da vida* grew directly out of his affection for the *sertanejo* music that he heard on the radio while on location in Mato Grosso in the interior of Brazil. When financial constraints forced him to abandon a film project about the Brazilian abolitionist poet Castro Alves, he decided to make a modest movie about this music, and he contracted Milionário and José Rico, the best-known *sertanejo* duo at the time, to play themselves in the film.

Like dos Santos's earlier films *Vidas secas* and *O amuleto de Ogum*, *Estrada da vida* focuses on rural migrants and their hopes for a better life in the city. But it is also a comedy that harks back to the *chanchada* tradition and shows the good-natured humor and innocence of provincial types in contrast to the often insensitive, rude, and even deceitful disposition of city dwellers. Chief among the latter is Malaquias (Raimundo Silva), a conniving, small-time agent renowned for bilking his clients, who books Milionário and José Rico as singers in a down-at-the-heels circus on the outskirts of São Paulo. The duo's slapstick-style humor here and elsewhere in the film evokes the comic routines of the great *chanchada* duo Grande Otelo and Oscarito. As they run to the circus tent's center stage, José Rico and Milionário are literally chased by Malaquias, who is irate because they wear street clothes instead of the gaudy costumes he associates with *dupla* performers. Malaquias has no knowledge of *sertanejo* music and he mistakes his new entertainers for a *caipira* (hillbilly) duo. (A bit later on, the team is also forced to correct the circus announcer, who mispronounces the name of the music they are about to play, a traditional form of country music called *modão*.) In the verbal exchange between the three men in front of the circus audience, José Rico and Milionário make Malaquias into the unwitting "burro" of their act, and he is laughed off the stage by an appreciative public.

As they break into song, José Rico notices that he has a giant hole in the toe of his shoe. Equally significant in this sequence is the attention dos Santos gives to the people in the audience. At one point, to stress the communal character of the musical show, the camera is set up behind the duo so as to view the spectators, and throughout the performance the film cuts back and forth between the faces of the musicians and the faces of their public. The technique spills over into a scene that occurs after the show, when the duo is again confronted by Malaquias, this time outside the circus tent. As in the earlier encounter, bystanders are filmed watching and listening as Malaquias shouts and shakes his fist at the two men, and once again dos Santos allows us to see the crowd's collective reaction to the comic exchange. As Malaquias stalks off, the amused bystanders disperse and a rooster crows derisively off-screen. These high jinks quickly subside when a recording company representative approaches Milionário and invites the pair to call at his studio. The sudden turn in fortune occurs as a young fan named Isabel (Sílvia Leblon), whom we have seen in the audience, shyly asks José Rico for a signed photograph. She reappears later in the film and shortly thereafter becomes his girlfriend.

Mr. Braulio, the owner of the small recording studio where José Rico and Milionário cut their first demo, seems unmoved by their music (when this pair enters a recording booth, we see another *dupla* act leaving it). Although he ultimately produces their record, he does nothing to capitalize on their talent. In one scene, he seems almost avuncular if not apologetic as he offers José Rico a loan when their record fails to be picked up by the radio stations. In two subsequent scenes, however, we see their music's strong appeal to a working-class audience. In the first of these scenes, José Rico and Milionário, who have day jobs as painters, stand on a scaffold near the top of a high-rise building and sing about their homeland as they work. The urban São Paulo landscape is suddenly transformed as if by magic into a lush, green rural setting. (Francisco de Assis, who wrote the screenplay, claims this was the first use of the matte system in a Brazilian movie [Salem 325]). Meanwhile, other workers stop to listen to the duo's song, which has a special utopian meaning for the migrant population. The construction foreman then fires Milionário and José Rico for the disruption, and they walk through the city looking for work.

Dos Santos remains true to his origins as a neorealist and documentary filmmaker during this part of the film, showing the two men as they pass by partially constructed and abandoned building sites. Here and elsewhere the film calls attention to the declining urban infrastructure and the consequent employment difficulties faced by city job seekers. Ultimately, Milionário and José Rico find short-term jobs painting in a record shop, and the actions in this sequence recall the earlier *chanchada*-like character of the tent scene. Standing on ladders and dressed in painters' overalls and newspaper hats, they notice their photograph on their record, which appears in the front of a display. Embarrassed by their current circumstances and anxious not to be recognized, José Rico climbs down the ladder, picks up all the copies of the record, and tries to hide them inside his overalls. As he climbs back up the ladder, the copies cascade onto the floor; the people in the store point and laugh while the irate store manager accuses them of theft. At this moment, an employee begins to play their record and everyone in the store listens. The employee recognizes them from the record cover, and the customers as well as the manager applaud them when the song ends.

The sense of community and well-being evoked here and in the earlier construction scene is repeated throughout the film; music becomes the agent of solidarity for a mostly marginalized population. For example, after another successful but unpaid performance in the countryside, José Rico and Milionário find themselves stranded without money or transportation back to the city. They sleep in a field (where a steer makes a meal of Milionário's only sport coat), and the next morning they feast on oranges from a grove for their breakfast. When they hear the crew picking oranges nearby, they offer to help by loading the crates of fruit onto a truck. Later in the day, the pair gets a ride in a large open-air truck and continues to pay for their breakfast by playing a *modão* while they travel cross-country. The entire sequence might be viewed as dos Santos's way of paying homage to the migrant labor force that is transported back and forth to the city. By showing the pair eagerly joining the crew and then serenading them with a song, he invests the scene with an energizing, uplifting force that emphasizes the spirit of community labor and solidarity.

The slightly Manichean approach to urban/rural characterizations in the first part of the film gradually recedes as the singing duo becomes more and more successful. In a scene reminiscent of numerous tales about strong religious beliefs of backlanders, José Rico takes Milionário to a church, where he asks the local patron saint, Nossa Senhora da Apareci-da (Our Lady of the Appeared), for her help. As a token of his apprecia-tion for listening to his request, he leaves a copy of their record near the church's altar. The record is discovered by a priest, who sends it to a near-by radio station, where it is played and becomes an instant success. As a result, the two musicians make other records with the same small-time record studio owner who had earlier seemed to have no confidence in their music, and they travel the country with Malaquias, who asks forgiveness for his past offenses and offers himself as their publicity agent.

Early in the film, we see Milionário and José Rico meeting one an-other in the shabby Hotel dos Artistas, where they are given rooms with little space and no view. After their celebrity is established, the hotel manager literally rolls out the red carpet and refurbishes an entire floor for them. He then turns the hotel into a small-time tourist attraction, wallpapering the modest lobby with publicity posters of the duo. Despite this new-found abundance, however, Milionário and José Rico manage to retain much of their innocence and their migrant character. They pur-chase a car and new clothes, but they remain rural folk at heart. This is particularly evident in their choice of wardrobe, which includes bulky gold chains and other jewelry, and José Rico's continuing religious faith. Com-plementing his Elvis-style sunglasses is a large gold cross that he wears on a chain around his neck, and at the beginning of each concert he gives thanks to the patron saint for granting his request for success.

Despite the common notion that you can't go home again after suc-cess, the pair does not stay in the big city. Tired of touring the country and longing for their families, Milionário and José Rico return to their homes in separate parts of the interior. (This nostalgia, however, does not apply to women in the story. Milionário's girlfriend, Madalena, who traveled to São Paulo from Minas Gerais, refuses to return and point-edly stays with José Rico's girlfriend, Isabel, in the city.) Toward the end of the film in a particularly impressive montage segment, the music of the duo accompanies the daily routines of men, women, and children from their early waking hours into their work day. This segment not only conveys the popularity of the two singers but also shows the potentially utopian force of a certain kind of grass-roots popular music, which provides an uplifting emotion for a community that lives at the low-income and poverty levels.

Estrada da vida offers a quite different view of the recording industry than what we see in dos Santos's earlier film, *Rio, Zona Norte*. In the latter film, a poor but talented black composer is forced to sell his sambas to others for little money so that they can be recorded, and in some instances the sambas are recorded without payment or permission. There is no happy ending in *Rio, Zona Norte*, nor does there appear to be any solution to the obstacles, dilemmas, and injustices encountered by poor and working-class musicians. In contrast, *Estrada da vida* treats Brazilian music with straightforward enthusiasm, and it shows a small record company that gives a singing duo a chance at modest success. Dos Santos also, and quite uncharacteristically, offers a happy ending, thus allowing the utopian quality of the music to remain in force. As a result, he creates a film that is entertaining without being false about social reality. *Estrada da vida* is one of the few pictures about music and show business that makes a utopia feel authentic.

A Return to Adaptation: *Memórias do cárcere, Jubiabá,* and *A terceira margem do rio*

On the face of it, *Estrada da vida* appears to have very little in common with dos Santos's next project—a highly ambitious three-plus-hour adaptation of Graciliano Ramos's two-volume *Memórias do cárcere* (Memoirs of Prison; 1953), which describes his imprisonment by the Vargas regime in the thirties. But according to dos Santos, *Estrada da vida* served as a proving ground or template for the kind of unmediated, nonjudgmental view of characters and social types that he hoped to achieve in his 1984 film (Salem 341). Consequently, instead of constructing the film along the lines of Ramos's first-person narrative, he merely shows Ramos alongside a range of other characters, many of whom, like him, are political prisoners. Ramos's writerly persona is remarkably quiet and subdued in the film, and his actions in the prison scenes are minimalist: we see him chain-smoking, drinking coffee, and jotting down ideas and impressions. At no point do we ever know what he is writing, although several prisoners say that they hope to be included in his book. This particular aspect of the film has a nice ironic touch—as if the story on the screen were somehow unrelated to what Ramos is writing throughout the movie. And yet there is a certain truth to the film's silence about Ramos as an author. In real life, Ramos was unable to take the manuscript with him when he was released from jail. His memoirs are therefore a reconstruction of the time he spent in prison that contains the names and descriptions of around three hundred inmates.

Ramos wrote *Memórias do cárcere* some ten years after the Vargas regime imprisoned him on suspicion of being a Communist. He was never formally charged, but he spent ten months being moved from one prison to another until his release in 1937. The world that he evokes in his memoirs is always restricted or contained, whether within the hold of a prison ship or within the walls of a penitentiary or within the fencing that rings the island penal colony. This sense of entrapment functions as a metaphor for a people that, at different points in history, was placed under lock and key by the government. Unfortunately, Ramos died before finishing the manuscript. But the book's open-endedness (not altogether unlike some of his fictional writings) does nothing to detract from the poignancy and magnitude of the story.

It took dos Santos two years just to prepare to write the script. During those years, he worked on cataloguing the characters, distilling the events, and formulating an ending for the film. He assembled a cast of some one hundred actors and filmed in three different locales: Maceió, the capital of Alagoas, where Ramos once lived; Campo Grande, where an outdoor penal colony was constructed; and on the island Ilha Grande. As dos Santos observed, it was not difficult to reproduce the look of thirties Brazil because, like much of the country, Campo Grande and Ilha Grande were relatively untouched by modernization. But the training of the large cast and the logistics of filming a project of this size without the benefit of a studio and on a budget of only $550,000 were daunting. (According to the film's producer, Luiz Carlos Barreto, every time the crew shot a sequence in Campo Grande, they had to stop the traffic on nearby roads so that the noise would not be picked up when they filmed [Salem 340].) All this work was worthwhile because dos Santos had wanted to make *Memórias do cárcere* ever since the military seized control of the government in 1964. With the political opening well underway in the early eighties, the time was right for a movie about the persecution of men and women who had resisted Vargas's regime—a situation that was all too familiar to liberal and left-wing groups in the years following the 1964 coup. As dos Santos remarks in an interview, "My idea was to make the film at the beginning of the [1964] dictatorship in order to say 'Beware of the dictatorship!' But I had to wait twenty years . . . to say: 'See what a horrible thing a dictatorship is?'" (qtd. in Amancio 76).

In formal terms, *Memórias do cárcere*, true to the spirit of Ramos, is a work of straightforward social realism; it is even less formally experimental than *Vidas secas*, which contains some rather stylized sequences as well as an overtly expressive soundtrack. There are no flashforwards or flashbacks and no story lines that alternate between past and present. The narrative is a slightly modified chronological history beginning shortly after the Left's attempted coup in 1935 and ending in 1937 with Ramos's release from prison. The only framing device is the soundtrack, on which the Brazilian national anthem plays at the beginning and end. This music deserves a brief comment because of the complex feelings that it evokes.

In the first minutes of the movie, we see Ramos (Carlos Vereza) being threatened by telephone calls and telegrams that disapprove of his actions as director of public instruction. (We learn in a later scene that he is being criticized for not permitting the state anthem to be played in public schools.) Below his office window, fascist Green Shirts break formation and give chase to government soldiers who have been watching and jeering at them. As the scene ends, the national anthem begins to play as nondiegetic background to the film's credits. Whether because of the particular part of the anthem that is being played or because of the atmosphere of expectation and tension that has been created in the precredits scene, the music has a disturbing if not ominous effect. As a march, it has an interesting relationship to the scene of the Green Shirts, who parade up and down in front of a government building; it seems almost wryly ironic in relation to a text that, appearing at the very beginning of the film, informs the viewer that Vargas has suspended all individual liberties.

The anthem appears again at the end of the movie, when Ramos is released from prison. The part of the score played here is more lighthearted and melodic, conveying a sense of tranquility that complements the look of relief on Ramos's otherwise gaunt and tired face. The music ultimately segues into the march we heard at the beginning of the film.

However, instead of accompanying a right-wing military formation, it is played as an ailing and aged Ramos slowly limps away from the prison gates—much like a wounded soldier coming home or a survivor emerging from a concentration camp. As his ship pulls away from the island prison, he tosses his hat into the air in a celebratory and liberating gesture. One can imagine the mixed emotions that the anthem evoked in Brazilian audiences who were themselves just beginning to experience a newfound freedom after twenty years of dictatorship.

Although dos Santos condenses the events in Ramos's book, he gives special attention in the first part of the film to the writer's state of mind prior to his imprisonment. Ramos's alienation is clearly expressed by his near indifference to the pressures and threats that he receives on the phone, in the mail, and in person. When his assistant rushes to his house to tell him that the police plan to arrest him, he receives the news with extraordinary calm, getting dressed in a suit, tie, and panama hat and patiently waiting with his wife and children in the family's parlor (see fig. 14). The camera pauses on this solemn family group, which is strangely still and silent. Because they are looking in the direction of the camera and are framed by an open parlor door, the overall effect is of a posed family photograph. When the police finally arrive, Ramos informs them politely, and to their surprise, that they are late. His alienation is so great that he makes no attempt to escape, nor does he ask the charge or plead his innocence. He merely accompanies the police and quietly follows instructions. Finally, he is taken to a prison ship bound for a penitentiary in Rio.

The first part of the film focuses entirely on the outward behavior of Ramos, who seems weary and vaguely resigned to being arrested. In fact, prior to his arrest Ramos confides to his assistant that he already feels as though he was in prison. However, when he arrives on the ship and descends into the dark hold, the film becomes more subjective, showing what the prisoner sees (and presumably will be writing about). His initial view of the ship's hold is a good example of prison seen through his eyes and is one of the most impressive shots in the film. The spectacle is Dantesque: a huge dark space crowded with bedraggled men and women of various ages who are sitting or slowly moving about. Row upon row of drooping hammocks hang from the ceiling, giving the ship's hold a strange and ghostly look. As Ramos descends the ladder and takes in

Figure 14. Glória Pires as Heloísa and Carlos Vereza as Graciliano Ramos in *Memórias do cárcere*. (Museum of Modern Art/Film Stills Archive)

the vision before him, he turns to another prisoner, a military officer, and asks if he has ever seen anything like it. The question is as much addressed to the audience as to the officer, who responds negatively and whose face registers utter disbelief.

In making the movie, dos Santos reduced the number of characters to one hundred, and around a dozen of those are given roles that lend a certain roundness to their characters or that establish them as representing specific types (see fig. 15). For example, there is the outgoing northeasterner, Mário Pinto (José Dumont), a political prisoner who loves to joke, sing, sleep around, and drink. His last wish as he lies dying from pneumonia is for a taste of *cachaça*, the cane liquor produced in the Northeast. There is also a former union official (Nildo Parente) who dons a silk smoking jacket and manages to have special meals prepared for him while in the penitentiary. Once on the island penal colony, his status changes radically. Although he requests light kitchen work, he is treated like all others who are fit and is sent to do backbreaking road work. Toward the end of the film he is stooped over with his smoking jacket wrapped around his head as protection from the sun. Another fascinating character is the misanthropic radical Soares, who is played by one

Figure 15. *Left to right:* Carlos Vereza, Nildo Parente, Jofre Soares as Soares, and José Dumont as Mário Pinto in *Memórias do cárcere*. (Museum of Modern Art/Film Stills Archive)

of dos Santos's favorite actors, Jofre Soares. A puritanical leftist and totalitarian, he accuses Ramos of being a capitalist simply because Ramos gives money to the wily Gaúcho (Wilson Grey), who has offered to sell the ailing writer a cot that he just seized when its former occupant was found dead. The misanthrope's rantings about Ramos's lack of egalitarianism continue unabated, even though Ramos has agreed to give the bed to someone sicker than he, and they bring about one of the writer's only outbursts. The scene is driven to a dramatic pitch as Ramos shouts at the recalcitrant militant, proclaiming with bitter irony that he is indeed guilty of being a *proprietário* (property owner). He then proceeds to settle himself onto the rickety cot that just minutes before had been the property of a dead man.

One of the most fascinating figures in the film is Gaúcho, who is imprisoned for being a thief. A tall, lanky character from the southernmost part of Brazil, he steals a stack of paper from the director's office so that Ramos can continue to write. His gesture earns him a beating and a long stay in solitary confinement. Reunited with his fellow prisoners toward the end of the film, he thumbs through a book on Ramos's cot and begins to read a passage about Zumbi, the legendary slave-turned-leader who founded a republic for runaway slaves in Palmares. (Although the title is never mentioned, the book Gaúcho is reading is Jorge Amado's *Jubiabá,* one of dos Santos's favorite novels of the thirties, which he adapted for the screen shortly after finishing *Memórias do cárcere.*) Other memorable characters include the compassionate Cuban prisoner-foreman (Waldyr Onofre), who tries to get the ailing Ramos to eat in exchange for which he will give him a small stack of paper. Another prisoner-employee, who is gay and sadistic, forces men entering the island colony to stand before him, strip, and relinquish their most cherished material possessions. (A more sympathetic view of homosexuality appears later in the film. Having received notice of his transfer from the colony, a highly distraught prisoner refuses to leave his lover and ends up attacking another prisoner with a shiv in order to remain on the island.)

The film pays equal attention to prison officials, among them the chief guard, Arruda (Jackson de Souza), who randomly beats prisoners and reminds them that they will all die on the island. But Arruda also displays a certain compassion for those who are ill, including Ramos, by allowing them to remain in the prison compound as opposed to forcing them to do manual labor outside the camp. At one point he approaches Ramos, whom he knows to be a writer, and asks him if he will write a speech for him to deliver on the prison director's birthday. Ramos politely informs the guard that, given the circumstances, it would be impossible for him to write such a speech. He asks Arruda if he were in Ramos's position, would he be able to write such a speech. A contemplative Arruda responds with a curt "no," but he is clearly not used to being turned down or humiliated. When Ramos appeals to Arruda to ask him to do something else, Arruda turns his back on Ramos and stalks off.

The director of the prison camp appears only at the end of the film, when Ramos is about to be released. He acts like a hotel manager who is eager to please his distinguished visitor and apologizes for any inconveniences. Ramos sheds his passive persona and demands that his personal possessions be returned to him. The director is offended by Ramos's accusation that anyone would steal from the prisoners and is undone when the prison employee who took Ramos's wallet and hat returns them, claiming that they had simply been misplaced. Ramos turns on the director and tells him that he will make public the sordid conditions of the prison once he is released. Although the director orders the confiscation of Ramos's manuscript, the Cuban foreman manages to aid Ramos once again by secretly handing each prisoner a few sheets of the manuscript, which they quickly conceal under their ragged clothing.

There are few women in the film, but their roles are as compelling as those of the men. At the beginning, Heloísa (Glória Pires), Ramos's young second wife, is viewed as a mother and a not very capable provincial housewife. When Ramos leaves for prison, he tells her to move in with her parents and sell the furniture should she need money. But Heloísa is not the fragile creature that Ramos believes her to be. She follows him from the Northeast to Rio, hires a lawyer, and makes the round of government offices, including the presidential palace, to argue for his release. She works with his publishers and even manages to throw him a party in the penitentiary when his newest book appears. She also assists other prisoners by smuggling letters and documents. We glimpse other women held in a common cell adjacent to the men's prison in Rio. According to Salem, dos Santos attempted to make the women prisoners seem strong by showing them as courageous and optimistic. Notice also that a general uproar among prisoners occurs when the news gets out that "Olga" has been deported to Germany. The reference here is to Olga Benário, one of the few historical figures mentioned by name in the film. Benário was a German Jew and Communist assigned by the Soviets to accompany the Communist leader Luís Carlos Prestes back to Brazil and who lived with Prestes until their arrest by the Vargas regime; her deportation to Germany was a death sentence and a major blow to the Left.

Memórias do cárcere was a success at the Cannes Film Festival, where it won the International Film Critics' Award. But the festival organizers did not include it among the movies to compete for the Palme d'Or, arguing that its lengthy running time made its participation prohibitive. In his favorable review, the French critic Louis Marcorelles described their action as an "aberration." Dos Santos faced a different set of problems when the film was released in Brazil. Attempting to capitalize on its success at Cannes and at the Havana Film Festival, where it received the prize for best film, the distributors not only set tickets prices higher but also forced anyone who wished to see to the movie to go to the Banco Nacional to buy tickets. Dos Santos spoke out against these tactics, observing that the capitalistic distributors were far more successful than the censors had ever been in keeping the public from seeing his film. Once these restrictive measures were removed, however, more than 1.5 million Brazilian tickets were sold; the film received international distribution and became a commercial as well as critical success in an otherwise bleak year for the Brazilian film industry.

In 1983, while working on *Memórias do cárcere*, dos Santos was approached by the French cultural minister Jack Lang about the possibility of coproducing a film. The following year, dos Santos, Louis Moillon, who was the head of Société Française de Production, and Embrafilme came to an agreement, and dos Santos began filming his adaptation of Jorge Amado's *Jubiabá*, a picaresque novel that draws heavily from a tradition of popular literature in Brazil known as *literatura de cordel* (chapbooks). Published in 1935, *Jubiabá* is one of Amado's most political works, and its protagonist, Antônio Balduíno ("Baldo"), is one of the first black heroes in Brazilian literature. The novel was the first to describe in rich detail the customs and religious practices of the poor and largely black community in Salvador, Bahia. It gives special attention to candomblé and to the role of the *pai-de-santo* (whose name in this case is Jubiabá). But unlike Amado's later novel, *Tenda dos milagres, Jubiabá* takes a strictly Marxist approach to religion, characterizing candomblé as an opiate. After a life of ups and downs as a street urchin, a boxer, a circus performer, and a worker in the cane fields, Baldo's political consciousness is raised when he joins forces with a group of dockworkers in a local strike. He quickly becomes a compelling spokesman who publicly criticizes the company bosses and capitalism in general, and he ultimately overshadows his mentor, Jubiabá, becoming the community's new leader and urging the people to come together and resist those who seek to keep them impoverished and silent.

Perhaps because he was no longer comfortable or in agreement with *Jubiabá*'s Marxist stance on religion, dos Santos preferred to focus on the book's love story between Baldo and Lindinalva, the white daughter of a well-to-do businessman who takes in the young Baldo when his only relative, a mentally unstable aunt, is committed to an asylum. When Baldo is wrongly accused by the family's bigoted housekeeper of sexually improper behavior toward Lindinalva, he is beaten by the father and runs away. From that point on, every woman he meets is a reminder of Lindinalva, whose unusual name is a combination of the words *pretty* and *white*. Unfortunately, the film, which was released in 1987, sacrifices a series of interesting characters and adventures in the book to focus on the love story. Not even the appearances of major actors such as Grande Otelo (who plays a less-than-convincing Jubiabá), Betty Faria, Zezé Motta, Ruth de Souza, and Jofre Soares can offset the film's often heavy-handed sentimentalism. When Jubiabá kneels in front of Baldo at the end of the film, there is no sense of the religious or political significance of the priest's unusual act. To his credit, however, dos Santos elaborates on the love story in the novel, showing both Baldo and Lindinalva longing for one another over the years and entirely eliminating Amado's stereotypical treatment of Baldo as a black man obsessed with whiteness.

Seven years separates *Jubiabá* from dos Santos's next film, *A terceira margem do rio* (The Third Bank of the River; 1994), which was co-produced with France. Although based on the story "A terceira margem do rio" by João Guimarães Rosa, one of Brazil's most distinguished writers, the movie incorporates ideas and characters from his other stories, including "A menina de lá" (The Girl from Beyond), "Os irmãos Dagobé" (The Dagobé Brothers), "Seqüência" (Cause and Effect) and "Fatalidade" (My Friend the Fatalist). Dos Santos uses the plot of "A terceira margem do rio" as the central impetus as well as frame for the other tales, which he strings together as episodes in the life of a backlander family.

As an adaptation of several separate and unrelated stories, the film is a tour de force. Dos Santos is also successful in recreating the supernatural or fairytale-like atmosphere of Rosa's backland world. His "A terceira margem do rio" centers on the relationship between a son, Liojorge (Ilya São Paulo), and a father who inexplicably leaves his family to spend his life paddling a canoe up and down a nearby river. The tale is one of many stories by Rosa in which he represents life in the backlands as mysterious, otherworldly, and riven with psychological drama. The first part of the film focuses on this story, showing the father's departure and the son's long-term devotion to his absent parent, even though he never actually sees his father on the river. The only evidence of the father's existence is an empty plate left on the riverbank, which the son dutifully refills with food each day. Rosa's original story has a far more troubling psychology. While the rest of the family moves to the city, the son remains behind, forsaking any future or happiness that he might have to stay close to his father. In the film, however, Liojorge leaves his riverbank home momentarily and follows a cow across the river. The cow leads him to Alva (Sonjia Saurin), the beautiful daughter of a rancher from the story "Seqüência," whom he marries and brings back to the family home. The film then segues into the plot of "A menina de lá," about a child named Nhinhninha (Bárbara Brandt) with magical powers, who is born to the young couple (see fig. 16). The son takes his bride and newborn daughter to the riverbank to introduce them to his absent father. His sister accompanies them and also calls out to her father, announcing her decision to live with her boyfriend; sometime later, she returns to call out to him that she is leaving for the city.

Dos Santos clearly makes important changes to the narrative by giving the son a wife and child. He also keeps the mother figure front and center, as opposed to following Rosa's narrative and allowing her to leave for the city. Dos Santos's casting of the photogenic and charismatic Maria Ribeiro, who appears as the mother in both *Vidas secas* and *O amuleto de Ogum,* was an especially wise move. Audiences immediately associate her with these earlier films, and there are moments when *A terceira margem do rio* actually pays tribute to her character in *Vidas secas,* showing her once again at the window of a house watching the rain fall on the drought-ridden land, smoking a pipe, and spitting on the ground. Like the character in *Vidas secas,* this mother speaks very little, but as in the earlier film Ribeiro's quiet demeanor lends her screen image power and presence.

The sudden appearance of the sinister Dagobé brothers, a roving band of toughs, one of whom has designs on Alva, causes the family to flee. Here the film takes an interesting turn from Rosa's narrative as it follows Liojorge and his wife, daughter, and mother to Brasília, where his sister and her husband now live. By moving the film from the countryside to the city, dos Santos sets up a contrast between the preindustrial Brazilian interior and the ultramodern world of the country's capital, with its superhighways and futuristic buildings. The family's home along the riverbank seems idyllic compared with their new residence in a dusty and overpopulated housing project in one of Brasília's frontier-style satellite communities. The tranquility of rural life vividly contrasts

Figure 16. Bárbara Brandt as Nhinhninha in *A terceira margem do rio*. (Nelson Pereira dos Santos collection)

with the violence of urban life, which is exacerbated by the almost magical reappearance of the Dagobé brothers. Continuing to taunt and threaten the family, one of the brothers manages to kidnap Alva. Liojorge takes vengeance by approaching a local assassin (Jofre Soares), a character from Rosa's story "Fatalidade," who helps him kill the kidnapper. Earlier in the film, the magical powers of the young couple's child, Nhinhninha, have become known to the townsfolk. She soon becomes a celebrity and a sort of commodity that helps to enrich the family. At the same time, the number of people who seek her out grows so great that she becomes weak from the work of bestowing blessings and dies.

The film ends with Liojorge back in the countryside, standing along the riverbank. He steps into the river, calls to his father, and offers to take his place in the canoe—an offer that harks back to his adolescent desire to accompany his father when he first left shore. To his complete amazement, the father and his canoe appear out of the mist. The implications of his offer suddenly frighten him, and he fights the river's current. Flailing his arms and struggling against the water's pull, he scrambles up the bank to safety. As the ghostly vision of his father recedes into the mist, he runs across the landscape, fleeing the reality and horror of the "third bank."

A terceira margem do rio addresses several topics treated in dos Santos's earlier films. Drought, for example, makes a brief appearance, although it merely provides an occasion for Nhinhninha to use her miraculous powers. What critics such as Stam refer to as the "magical realist" aspects of the film, based primarily on the actions of the daughter, have an antecedent in *O amuleto de Ogum,* where the spiritual world, in the form of an amulet, protects Gabriel from physical harm. Like *Vidas secas* and *O amuleto de Ogum,* the film also describes the migration of rural dwellers to the city. However, unlike the family in *Vidas secas,* the protagonists in *A terceira margem do rio* do not flee for economic reasons; the countryside is not at all impoverished or uninhabitable, but rather a *locus amoenus* that the family is forced to flee because of the Dagobé brothers. While offering a very different view of the countryside, dos Santos also makes a powerful statement on city life and the nature of progress and modernization when he films the family's arrival in the violent and crowded settlement in Brasília. The son's arrest and imprisonment by the police is also reminiscent of the unjust treatment of Fabiano in *Vidas secas;* but while Fabiano demurs from taking vengeance on his persecutor, Liojorge uses his prison contacts to meet with a hit man who helps him murder his nemesis.

A terceira margem do rio resembles dos Santos's previous work in its approach to religion and spirituality. For example, shortly after the father's departure in his canoe, the puzzled and chagrined family members arrange for a priest to carry out an exorcism—as if the father's inexplicable act were somehow the work of the Devil. Throughout, the family and the largely migrant community in Brasília make virtually no distinction between formal religion and the more general belief in the supernatural. Like Fátima, the young daughter becomes a magnet for hundreds of believers who bring offerings so as to be heard and receive the child's blessing. The scene in which she dispenses an endless supply of sweets to neighborhood children is endearing, but when the townsfolk become aware of her powers, she is dressed in white and placed on a raised platform, where she receives and responds to an ever-growing community in need.

Unlike Carlos Diegues's *Bye Bye Brasil* (1983), which follows a young rural couple and their child traveling about the countryside and finally making good in Brasília, dos Santos's film destroys any notion that the city is the promised land of the migrant. In keeping with Rosa's fictional works, dos Santos privileges the countryside over the city, treating the Brazilian backlands not as a socioeconomic reality but rather as a utopian myth. His characters, imbued with a sense of wonder, mystery, and magic, struggle between the forces of good and evil, but at the same time we can see how those forces relate to everyday social realities.

Melodrama and Cinema Novo: *Cinema de lágrimas*

Shortly after completing *A terceira margem do rio,* dos Santos began work on a project for the British Film Institute to commemorate the centenary of cinema. The BFI had commissioned nearly twenty directors worldwide to make movies that would portray the history of cinema in their respective countries, but instead of recognizing Latin America as a large and highly diverse geographic region made up of different countries, languages, and cultures, it chose to regard the region as a homogeneous entity. As dos Santos points out, a history of Latin American cinema as a whole would have required at least a four-hour film (Amancio 81). While the BFI gave him complete freedom to take whatever approach he wanted, a four-hour documentary was out of the question.

Yet perhaps the impossibility of representing all of Latin American cinema forced dos Santos to think about the project in a totally new way. Instead of filming a documentary survey, which was the approach taken by the majority of directors in the series, he decided to make a dramatic film about the Golden Age of Latin American melodrama—a genre that had thrived in countries such as Mexico and Argentina from the thirties until the fifties. The project was inspired by the book *Melo-*

drama: Um cinema de lágrimas da América Latina (Melodrama: A Cinema of Tears from Latin America; 1992) by the film scholar Sílvia Oroz, which surveys the history and success of what was often referred to as *filmes para chorar* (films to cry at).

Dos Santos used the book as an archival basis for his fictional film about an aging, homosexual Brazilian actor-playwright named Rodrigo (Raul Cortez) who is obsessed with a recurring dream about a childhood trauma—the suicide of his mother. To understand the mother's act, he decides to find the movie that she saw shortly before killing herself. The search takes him and a young research assistant (André Barros) from Rio to Mexico City, where they spend several days viewing clips of Mexican and Argentinian melodramas in the cinematheque at the Universidad Nacional Autónoma de México (UNAM). Perhaps as a result of the melodramatic romance and passion that he sees on the screen, Rodrigo ends up falling in love with his young assistant. But the assistant does not return Rodrigo's affection; he comes late to work, he repeatedly asks Rodrigo for money, and he is clearly harboring a secret. As the older man sits captivated by the projected drama and romance, the assistant takes a seat in the back row and reads aloud (to Rodrigo's dismay) from notes that he has written on the melodrama that tend to focus on the role of women and the theme of love.

Like the characters in the melodramas they watch, the actor and his assistant are caught up in a story of unrequited love, tragedy, and loss. After rebuffing Rodrigo's amorous attentions, the young man finally leaves him in Mexico. Later, the young man writes from his hospital deathbed, telling the actor that he is terminally ill, that he is a fugitive from drug traffickers and the police, and that by the time Rodrigo receives his letter he will be dead. He also writes that he finally located the long-sought melodrama, which he has copied and sent to Rodrigo on video. The film, *Armiño negro* (Black Ermine; 1953) by Carlos Hugo Christensen, an Argentinian, is a tragic tale about a young boy who kills himself after having learned that his mother is a prostitute. After viewing the video, Rodrigo realizes that his own mother decided not to risk the possibility of a similar disclosure and ended her life.

In *Cinema de lágrimas,* dos Santos returns to the popular theme of the mother-son relationship that appears as a subplot in his first film, *Rio, 40 graus.* But his approach in this case is very different. *Rio, 40 graus* is a left-wing film that uses what might be regarded as melodramatic emotion (in the broadest sense of the term) to criticize an oppressive class structure and to create sympathy for a large population that is struggling to survive. Dona Elvira, the maternal figure in that film, is a model of strength and virtue whose love and support for her son are unconditional. Although there are certain affinities between her character and the long-suffering mother figure made famous by Sara García in Mexican melodramas, she is portrayed as neither martyr nor victim. Despite her poverty and ill health, she is a conscientious mother and community member who accepts the kind acts of neighbors with grace and stands up to the authorities to keep an orphaned child out of the clutches of a dubious justice system. *Cinema de lágrimas,* on the other hand, uses middle-class characters to explore the psychology of the mother-son relationship and the mother's enduring presence in the son's life. The film begins with the actor's dream about his mother, and although this dream is not explicitly sexual, it prepares us for an Oedipal quest into the "maternal" element of cinema.

In some ways, the dream sequence has affinities with Buñuel's *Los olvidados,* in the sense that both movies feature sons who have conflicted relationships with their mothers and who dream about them approaching their beds. Buñuel, however, is explicit in his portrayal of Oedipal desire and much more unsettling in his use of a piece of glistening raw meat to suggest the mother's sexuality; his surrealistic approach to the dream creates a sense of strangeness and deep unease that inhibits any feeling of pathos. Dos Santos, by contrast, remains closer to the nexus of melodramatic emotions, juxtaposing the son's dream of his mother's tearful bedside farewell with his adult fascination for movies that feature women as wives and mothers in distress. Rodrigo's search through the cinematic archive is the very stuff of melodrama, replete with a family secret, a suicide, a case of unrequited love, a fateful letter that contains the answer to a riddle, and the death of a love interest. What is particularly interesting about this last aspect of the film is that dos Santos has changed the classic melodramatic formula about heterosexual relationships into a drama about homosexual love. Although Rodrigo repeatedly asserts that women were the primary audience for the old melodramas, we see him enjoying the old movies and even becoming teary-eyed.

The actor's search through the archive is also, of course, a fictional device that allows dos Santos to show brief clips, most of them in pristine condition, of wonderfully evocative black-and-white films of the studio era. By this means he pays tribute to a generation of directors, cinematographers, and stars who became internationally famous largely because of their work in melodramas. Although the content of these films had little to do with the social reality of the moviegoing public, the Mexican melodramas were among the highest-quality films made in Latin America. In effect, dos Santos, who began his career as a neorealist and a symbol of the Latin American New Wave, takes a revisionary approach to a genre that, like the Brazilian *chanchada,* was often criticized by the Left because of its association with Hollywood. He is particularly adept at showing how melodramas can continue to enthrall viewers like Rodrigo, who is visibly caught up in the films. As the critic Jésus Martín-Barbero notes:

> The melodrama was the dramatic backbone of all the plots, bringing together social impotency and heroic aspirations, appealing to the popular world from a "familiar understanding of reality." The melodrama made it possible for film to weave together national epics and intimate drama, display eroticism under the pretext of condemning incest, and dissolve tragedy in a pool of tears, depoliticizing the social contradictions of daily life. The stars—María Félix, Dolores del Río, Pedro Armendáriz, Jorge Negrete, Ninón Sevilla—provided the faces, bodies, voices and tones of expression for a people to see and hear themselves. Above and beyond the make-up and the commercial star industry, the movie stars who were truly stars for the people gathered their force from a secret pact that bonded their faces with the desires and obsessions of the publics. (365)

Among the Mexican melodramas that dos Santos includes in *Cinema de lágrimas* are early examples, such as *Santa* (Saint; 1931) by Antonio Moreno and *La mujer del puerto* (Woman of the Port; 1933) by Arcady Boytler. Later melodramas shown in the film include Julio Bracho's *Distinto amanecer* (A Different Dawn; 1943) with Pedro Armendáriz and Dolores del Río (both of whom were also under contract in Hollywood); Emilio Fernández's *Las abandonadas* (1944); films such as Roberto Gavaldón's *La diosa arrodillada* (The Kneeling Goddess; 1947) and Tito Davidson's *Doña Diabla* (Madame Devil; 1949), both of which feature the Mexican diva María Félix; and Luis Buñuel's surrealistic rendition of Brontë's *Wuthering Heights,* entitled *Abismos de pasión* (Abysms of Passion; 1953).

But *Cinema de lágrimas* also contains many references to Cinema Novo, which it often juxtaposes with the melodramas. Throughout the film, dos Santos points in various ways to the archival coexistence of the two forms: he incorporates bits and pieces from a UNAM professor's classroom lectures on Glauber Rocha and Cuban "imperfect cinema"; he slowly pans down hallways decorated with publicity posters of Cinema Novo productions; and he focuses on banners outside the cinematheque that refer to Cinema Novo. In the movie's final scene, Rodrigo wanders from a screening of *Armiño negro,* the film associated with his mother, into a screening of Glauber Rocha's *Deus e o Diabo na terra do sol,* which he views with students in a large auditorium (see fig. 17).

The political films of the sixties and seventies serve as a counterpoint to the various melodramas. One might say that dos Santos's film is an attempt to understand Latin American cinema in terms of a dialectic between two different moments in film history and two very different kinds of movies, one of which (melodrama) was highly successful with audiences at home and the other of which (Cinema Novo) was more popular with and better received by audiences abroad. He does not appear to privilege one over the other, and he even suggests that there are affinities between them. Dos Santos's homage to Rocha in the final scene is especially interesting in this regard. The clip he selects is from the end of the movie, beginning with the *cangaceiro* Corisco and his lover, Dadá, who are caught in a moving and tender embrace. The nondiegetic music is not all that different from the music one hears in the older melodramas, and it heightens the drama of the passionate scene. The next bit of film is of the hired gun, Antônio das Mortes, shooting the messianic Corisco while the film's lovers Manuel and Rosa race across the *sertão* to reach the sea. Like all of Rocha's work, the action here is highly theatrical and stylized, even if it does not have the slick look of the older studio productions. Dos Santos invites the viewer to ask exactly how Rocha's death scene differs in kind from, say, the dramatic death scene in Buñuel's *Abismos de pasión,* in which a lovesick and crazed Alejandro-Heathcliff is shot in the eye as he leans back against his beloved's open coffin. Isn't the race by the couple away from the vil-

Figure 17. Raul Cortez as Rodrigo watching
Glauber Rocha's *Deus e o Diabo na terra do
sol* in *Cinema de lágrimas*. (Museum of Modern
Art/Film Stills Archive)

lainous Antônio das Mortes and across the *sertão* as melodramatic as any
escape scene from the older movies? The points of contact between the
two forms seem even clearer as we watch Rodrigo looking at the Rocha
film and realize that his tearful yet pleasurable reaction to *Deus e o Di-
ablo na terra do sol* is not unlike his response to the melodrama. Both
types of films evoke a kind of historical nostalgia and pride.

Cinema de lágrimas is a minor work in dos Santos's career, but it
provides a complex and intelligent evolution in perspective. It synthe-
sizes the opposed qualities that make up his films (entertainment and
self-reflexive experiment, emotion and social critique), reconciling the
conflict between them. It serves also as a kind of retrospective of his art,
which, as we have seen, involves much of Brazilian film history. Dos
Santos was born into a direct experience of the entertainment cinema,
but his early work embraced the revolutionary potential of neorealism.
He inspired the Cinema Novo movement and made radical, allegorical
films that challenged the status quo. Later, he produced realist pictures
about popular culture, blending the traditions of documentary and en-

tertainment. In other words, he is a remarkably versatile director who has been open to new ideas and changing historical circumstances even while he has retained a commitment to the ordinary working life of Brazilians. A film like *Cinema de lágrimas* enables us to see where he has been and to look forward to where he will go.

Notes

1. With this title dos Santos is making a comparison between Freyre's importance and that of the Portuguese navigator Pedro Álvares Cabral, who "discovered" Brazil in 1500.

2. This and other translations from the Portuguese are my own.

3. In his study *Cinema: Trajetória no subdesenvolvimento* (Cinema: A Trajectory within Underdevelopment), the film historian and critic Paulo Emílio Salles Gomes calls attention to the social and historical importance of the *chanchada*, which was the country's only sustained alternative to Hollywood movies for two decades, and he praises it as a uniquely Brazilian form.

4. As Mariarosaria Fabris notes in *Nelson Pereira dos Santos: Um olhar neorealista?* (Nelson Pereira dos Santos: A Neorealist Gaze?), Vera Cruz was never concerned with the distribution and exhibition aspects of filmmaking. The company basically assured its financial downfall by giving Columbia Pictures and Universal International the rights to distribute its films (43).

5. See, for example, *Fundamentos,* Jan. 1951.

6. Dos Santos left the Communist party in 1956.

7. Readers should consult both Johnson, *Cinema,* and Stam for their extensive commentaries on this film.

8. In a 2001 interview, dos Santos stated that at the time he initially thought the camera work would resemble that of the Mexican master Gabriel Figueroa. But, he says, "'knowing my intentions to show the true *sertão,* [Barreto] decided to remove the filters and leave the lens bare'" (qtd. in Margarido 2).

9. According to dos Santos, Ramos was quite explicit about any changes made to his work. In his letter to dos Santos, he wrote: "'In my work, it's like this; if you do what you intend, then it's your work and not mine'" (qtd. in Margarido 2).

10. After the film was released, Alex Viany wrote that *El justicero* might be regarded as the third film in dos Santos's once projected (but never completed) trilogy about Rio. See *Jornal do Brasil,* Oct. 4, 1967.

11. In a 2001 interview, dos Santos remarked that he now considers *Fome de amor* his favorite film: "'It was the work in which I most let myself go, in which I managed best to bring about a new language. I wanted to free myself from the previous film; I needed that. I was a rebellious youth and I wanted to transgress'" (2). For a detailed critical discussion of this film, see Johnson, *Cinema* 183–89.

12. See, for example, "Como era gostoso o meu francês," *O globo,* 1 July 1972.

13. For more a detailed discussion of the economic ups and downs during the late sixties and early seventies, see Skidmore, *Politics of Military Rule.*

14. During a 2000 retrospective of dos Santos's films in Japan, the film was banned because of its scenes of nudity.

15. In a 1977 interview for the *Folha de São Paulo,* dos Santos looked back on the film's reception, stating: """The public didn't identify with my ideas. For example, they identified with the Frenchman, the colonizer. Everyone was saddened by the death of the 'hero.' They were so influenced by John Wayne 'bang-bangs' that they didn't understand that the hero was the Indian and not the young fellow""" (qtd. in Salem 267).

16. Embrafilme's initial mission was to help distribute Brazilian films worldwide. After its reorganization in 1975, the state organization became involved in all aspects of local filmmaking and, as John King notes, ultimately assumed total control over the industry (115). Randal Johnson writes that in 1975, Embrafilme's budget rose from 6 million to 80 million *cruzeiros,* or about U.S. $10 million (*Film* 138). For a detailed study of Embrafilme and the film industry in Brazil, see Johnson, *Film.*

17. As Jean-Claude Bernardet observes in his important essay "O amuleto mudou tudo" (The Amulet Changed Everything):

> Naturally, by not addressing the movie-going audience but rather the people, Nelson is making a choice: he is directing himself to that part of society that does not constitute the regular movie public.
>
> . . . After seeing *O amuleto,* one can no longer talk about film like before. *O amuleto* links film production to the people. Even for those who do not agree with Nelson's objectives, *O amuleto* establishes the grounds for further discussion. *O amuleto* proposes a drastic reformulation of the relations between filmmaker (and the intellectual in general) and the people. (11–12)

18. Arcanjo's story is loosely based on the life of the activist Manuel Querino.

GERALD O'GRADY: Cinema provided us with the enhanced power to record and capture exteriors. Yet, from the outset, you have been interested in exploring the interior, the mind, and I would ask you to reflect upon that impulse and the difficulties which you encountered.

NELSON PEREIRA DOS SANTOS: My way of making movies is to try to communicate what's going on inside the character . . . the thought, the feeling. It was born of a challenge created by literature. I'm very much in love with this, understand. So I thought that I could try the same thing with films. Cinema was limited to the concrete. It was difficult to get to the psychological, to the inside, except by using the device of the voiceover. . . . I thought that this was a rather literary device, a return to the days of radio. The action depended on the words spoken. To avoid this artifice is really a challenge.

I think that I had two great literary lessons: the first came from the literature that inspired me a lot. When making *Rio, 100 Degrees* [*Rio, 40 graus,* 1956], I borrowed the narrative construction of James Joyce's

Ulysses [1922] and created one day in Rio de Janeiro with many characters and children wandering around the city. But I didn't manage to represent the desired level of consciousness within them. It's all like a mosaic, a mosaic of the city, of its inhabitants, of what they could be thinking or dreaming. There is a little of the interior, yes, but not as much as in *Rio, Northern Zone* [*Rio, Zona Norte,* 1957], because the latter concentrates on only one character, the samba composer who suffers an accident that leaves him on the brink of death in a coma. As a result, we see him remembering the most significant moments of his life and thinking of what he should have decided in terms of a life plan. Because of this, it became easier to reproduce the inner state of the character. There was only one character, and this facilitated the construction of the film.

The other great lesson was a literary challenge and a rather well-known one: *Barren Lives* [*Vidas secas,* 1963]. When I proposed to adapt the novel, I received several warnings: "You will never be able to do the scene with Baleia (the dog), because it is not the consciousness of a human being. It is the consciousness of a dog. How will you convey what Graciliano Ramos wrote?" He lends, he attributes a psychology to the animal, to the bitch Baleia. Each moment that she participates in the life of the family, she has her own universe and her own vision, which the writer describes with great precision and affection. And I felt obligated to do this on film. And it was really a great challenge. Baleia exists as a character with an inner life and not only as an animal that passes through each scene once. And her presence is felt until the climax of the film—her death. She lives this scene as if she were a human.

In a situation where the characters try to express their sentiments, I worry about the line of thought. When a film has something to say, the dramatic conflict occurs on the level of ideas, of thought. It's not only in human relationships, love, conflicting interests, social conflicts, moral conflicts, but also on the level of ideas, how ideas are related, how they enter into conflict with other ideas. For example, the film [*Memoirs*] *of Prison* [*Memórias do cárcere,* 1984] is a work built more on the character's thought than on the relationships he has within the jail. The relationships he has within the jail are very common, the everyday life of a prisoner. The relationship with his wife is limited. Almost commonplace. But his thought process is as if he is going on a great journey or participating in a great story. It's similar to the type of dangerous trip to hell, passing by places that are striking to the character, and this sensation is reflected in his perception of the prisoners who come and go. So from the subjective point of view he is like Ulysses. The character is a man from the interior. In prison he will face and come to know true and false revolutionaries. He will come to know what he had never seen before, and everything that goes on inside himself, and the events in which he participates he analyzes according to his first vision, with the initial and original viewpoint of a man from the countryside. This is the idea of [*Memoirs*] *of Prison:* a trip along the mental plane.

GO: I would ask you to go further now and talk about the compositional elements of your films. You are almost unique as a major director because you have been involved in all phases of the filmmaking process: writing and designing your scripts and developing new directions in camera, lighting, and sound. Would you begin with the relation of script-writing to shooting?

NPS: All my films are about 50 percent a script which I came up with, wrote, imagined, scripted, etc., and the other 50 percent is improvisation. I think that improvisation always happens in my films, ever since the first one that had a very rigorous script, where everything was very well defined, like René Clair's iron script. Even with that script, I still managed to improvise. Improvisation is present in my work because of my education; this includes the documentaries, where one must invent a lot as well. The documentary didn't have a script so I had a lot of liberty, and it also had a lot of spontaneity in the placement of the camera. This was the training that I got from the documentary and from *Rio, 100 Degrees,* my first film, which had a strong documentary aspect to it and which was basically filmed on location, with a few exceptions. Many times the filming demands rapid solutions because of the light, so I was always obliged to improvise.

Hunger for Love [*Fome de amor,* 1967] is an example of total improvisation, the exaggeration of improvisation. Really, there was no script. It was a story that I didn't like, but the producer gave me carte blanche to do whatever I thought best. When I began the first day of shooting, I didn't know what I was going to shoot. I shot a take with a piano on top of a ferry in the middle of the ocean. I couldn't not shoot this image. During *Hunger for Love,* I made my first trip to the United States and I came in contact with underground production. The year was 1966.

Everything was in great turmoil—the war in Vietnam, young people burning their draft cards, drugs, protests at the universities, and the young people ready for a fight. It was a moment in which it was necessary to break with convention and to bring about a definite break. So *Hunger for Love* is the freest film I ever made.

What I would do every day was write for the actors. I didn't have a script for the whole film. I would make up a story as it was filmed. [Alexandre] Astruc said that the camera is like a pen. To write with the camera is what I did with *Hunger for Love*. There were several conditions I had to respect, among them, the actors—Leila [Diniz], Arduíno [Colasanti], Irene Stefânia, Paulo Porto—who were already under contract—and also the location—Angra dos Reis, the sea, the islands. I had to combine whatever came into my imagination with these fixed elements. The variables came from my imagination; the constants were the actors.

It's the same with popular songs—the singers, improvisation—someone starts a motif and the singer has to work with the motif, invent, imagine, but he has to respect the motif that is already there. *Hunger for Love* was an improvisation. The story in the book is the story of a pianist who goes to Paris and finds a teacher there. She gets to know him and that's a totally different story—it's romantic, it's music and love, something like that. There was a piano that the producer sent, a house on an island, there were actors, but I made it up. I changed the location from Paris to New York; I said, no, she lives in New York. I completely changed everything, even the essence of the story. The book is part of the motif, of course, since it was because of the book that the producer contracted the actors and sent the piano.

[*Memoirs*] *of Prison* took a long time to be made, because it had a great relationship, a very important one, with the life of the country itself, with the politics in Brazil, with the moment we were going through, and because of this the script had to be very well thought out. It also took a long time to make. I spent years working on the adaptation, on the script.

The script for [*The*] *Third Bank* [*of the River*] [*A terceira margem do rio*, 1994] is one that I didn't manage to film completely. The movie is a long way from the script in its setting and adaptation. I like both films, which are a consequence of my relationship with literature. It's like I managed to make an appropriation of the author. It was like the one who wrote either [*Memoirs*] *of Prison* or *Barren Lives* wasn't Graciliano. I appropriated those books because of my admiration for the work of the writer; by way of my profound connection with them, I discovered that I was the owner of the story. I think this is what happens in any adaptation. There was a time when I received many proposals to make films based on literary works but I didn't feel right and I refused many of them, because there must be a strong relationship beforehand between what I live and think and what I propose to do with a book and an author.

GO: I hope that you will now move to your "camera-ization" of some different scripts, as your camera itself seems to be a protean character.

NPS: Well, what precedes my work with the camera is the editing. When I'm writing, it is common for me to think about the editing, because while I'm filming, I'm also working on my editing project. All of my camerawork is done thinking about what will be possible when I edit and what changes in language, expression, and narrative there will be. I also film by thinking about possible alterations in structure and plot. So I film with great freedom. My camera is very free; I film a movement, and then in my head I erase that movement. It's not going to be there when it's edited. I work with a very thought-out structure for each sequence, but I am always thinking of other possible solutions.

I began to film at a time when there wasn't any video. Today it's possible to immediately see the result of what was shot, what the camera is seeing. In my training as a director, we had to wait a day to see the results of what the camera was seeing, of what was being filmed and recorded. And so there was the need for many other options, because we didn't know exactly if that actor's look was really there on the negative. In a few films I was able to set the camera so as to see the action from a distance. In that case the work process is different. . . . I create a reality with the actors and my camera films that as if it were the truth, as if all the action were reality. The camera has a quasi-documentary distance. This was the case in *How Tasty Was My Little Frenchman* [*Como era gostoso o meu francês,* 1972]. So many people thought that the Indians were real, that the hut and everything were real, because the camera had that distance of a foreigner, of someone who arrived to observe, an anthropologist, an ethnologist, or a reporter, a journalist, an onlooker. During shooting, when inventing all of that, building all that, I pretend that it is happening. When everything approaches what we can consider to be real, then I film. *Rio, Northern Zone* is not like this. It has this duality of a documentary when the police arrive and the guy falls off the train; these are the intervals between the flashbacks of the hero, who's in a coma. So the camera has its heroes. When the film follows the central character, it's an intimate camera; it's living his whole psychological universe.

In *The Amulet of Ogum* [*O amuleto de Ogum,* 1975] the camera is a believer. It believes; it's not a documentary camera. It is in agreement with the whole universe of popular religion, of the hero, of the closed body. It's an accomplice. It believes in that, it believes in everything, it doesn't have a distanced view. *The Road of Life* [*Estrada da vida,* 1981] is also very distanced but very tender—I mean, it has a very tender point of view. It is very sympathetic; it accepts what happens, but it doesn't get to the point of being an accomplice. But it has a point of view that is very important. *The Road of Life* has nothing documentary-like about it, but the camera is in a place that the characters like, or that I imagine the characters would like it to be. It gave the floor to the characters, I served them in this sense, so they could tell their own story. [*Memoirs*] is not a documentary. In [*Memoirs*], the camera is linked to the intelligence of the character[s], placed in relation to [them]. It's always very agile, very interested, curious, observing many characters, occurrences that are symbolic of the main character. The position of the camera is determined by what the character is thinking. In the prologue, Graciliano Ramos says the following: "I'm going to be obligated many times to use this abominable pronoun, which is the first person singular, but I promise the reader that I will hide behind it in order to better observe others." So this is the basic determinant for making [*Memoirs*] *of Prison.* I'm going to tell you the truth. Until I understood this, I couldn't make the film. I couldn't write the script, but when I suddenly discovered this, I said, "Ah, here it is." Because it was a story with a subjective camera. Few films have been made entirely with a subjective camera. And there is also the voiceover, explaining, informing us about the image that is happening. Graciliano gave me this great insight, because the whole film is like this. He's always present, but the camera is him and at the same time it isn't. What I mean is that he's hiding behind this "I," and he sees many things outside of himself with great liberty, and the other characters are presented to the camera, which isn't him. It's him, in the position of the narrator, because the whole book is narrated in the first person, but the camera isn't the first person. It's the mediation of the first person with others, with the Other.

GO: As lighting is one of your central compositional elements, one which is often insufficiently and inadequately commented upon, I would again ask you to provide us with some very specific information about your use of it, for example, in *Barren Lives.*

NPS: Well, to tell you the truth, in my films, in the first films, the lighting was simply whatever was possible. We would go to Sugarloaf, there was fog, and we would have to wait for a sunny day to film whatever was possible, because on these locations, it was impossible to control things and establish a lighting style. The technical result was acceptable, but we still didn't have the conditions to think about imposing a clear idea of the lighting.

The first time that I was able to employ a clear idea of lighting was in *Barren Lives.* This was [Luiz Carlos] Barreto's contribution. He was a follower of the [Henri] Cartier-Bresson school of thought, as was Zé Medeiros. Both of them were coming from *O cruzeiro* magazine, and they brought with them the great contribution of European photography to Brazilian cinema, which until then had been mostly based on American cinema. Of course, there was the school of the Mexican [Gabriel] Figueroa, those clouds and so on. Luiz Carlos Barreto brought the light of Cartier-Bresson to *Barren Lives.* It was a shocking experience, revolutionary, radical, to film without a filter, with a naked lens, to shine the light directly on the characters' faces. This was a great experience because that strong northeastern light demanded that every photographer who worked there place a filter on [the] lens to reduce the light, to reduce the light in general, on the actor's face. This, in turn, required the actor's face to be artificially lit. And because there weren't any large generators out in the backlands to make some heavy 5K, 10K reflectors and so on, we always used a portable reflector, which is a square with silver paper that reflects the sunlight but also carries that silver color, and no actor can manage to open his [or her] eyes (laughs), and then the clouds appear, which in fact makes you work backwards. In a situation like that, the best place to film is where there's less light on the actor's face, which is what you're photographing, and the rest comes as it will. In this circumstance, the director is forced to think about the miseen-scène in relation to photography; the light determines where the actors place themselves, where the characters place themselves, within a whole range of shades from black to white, all the way to that washed-out white in the background. One needs to see if a particular scene can be done with the trees there, the brush, the bushes, those obstacles, that dazzling light. This gives the film, the photography, very beautiful moments like a woodcarving, within the black and white—from total black to total white, this combination of black and white, beautiful grays—really, this was a lot of work. It wasn't done with artificial light; it was done with God's light. The interiors of the houses, all the interiors were lit only with natural light, the light that came in the windows, the doors. The light of a prison at nighttime, fire, a little fire that lit up the characters' faces . . . everything was done according to the lighting, which is essential to the final expression of the film. I don't think anything like this film had been done until then.

GO: Perhaps *Barren Lives* would also be a good film to ask you to talk about your use of sound.

NPS: I think that *Barren Lives* is an example of good sound work. I like it. I like to work with direct sound. There are few films that I dubbed in afterwards. When I'm filming I work with my ears too, not just with my eyes. I work while listening to what is happening, what noises are going on beneath the dialogue, at that moment in that scene. Working on external shots, in the country, there are birds that sing from far away, and there's always a combination, a relationship between the background noise and the text. For me, direct sound is fundamental. Just like the image, I have the sound. Of course all this sound will be worked on later. We always record more so we can add on, mix with the basic sound. In [*Memoirs*] *of Prison*, which doesn't have a single word dubbed in, everything was direct sound and background, but then the time came to put in some music. We didn't know what music—for me the sound in the film was finished, but we had to put in music. We had the same problem that we had with *Barren Lives*. In *Barren Lives*, there was some dubbing—there was direct sound, but a little dialogue was dubbed in, although the ambient sound, the backlands, was all recorded. I never thought about music for *Barren Lives*. For the music I used the sound of an oxcart, which is a sound integrated with that image. I couldn't think about music for that film.

GO: Thus far, we have talked about the compositional qualities, the aesthetics and artistry of cinema, but in all cases, particularly your own, these forms are always conditioned, to say the least, by the funds available for production. Here, your own struggle has great significance for world cinema, I think, and I would like to ask you to tell us about the details of that history.

NPS: Of the sixteen feature-length films that I've made, there's a lot of differences in the type of production from one to the next. For example, the first two, *Rio, 100 Degrees* and *Rio, Northern Zone,* were produced without any assistance, without any government money, nothing. It was an invention. I applied a formula that existed in cinema in Rio, which was the cooperative, where the actors and technicians work to receive a percentage, which means the right to share the profits in proportion to the value of their labor, in relation to the overall cost of the film. So let's say the film costs 100, the director's value is calculated at 10, so the director would get 10 percent of the film's earnings, and out of the rest, part of it would cover the labor costs, and the cash flow was covered by quotas that were sold. These quotas are sold to friends, to relatives, etc., to be invested in the film. So *Rio, 100 Degrees* was made this way and *Rio, Northern Zone.* The second was also helped by the cash prizes which I had received for *Rio, 100 Degrees,* and that helped produce Robert Santos's film, *O grande momento* [*The Great Moment*]. It was a whole economy, half volunteer, half the investment of shares. What happened is that *Rio, Northern Zone* and *O grande momento* were both failures at the box office and this experience died there. So I ended up owing a lot of money, and it was difficult to get it back.

On the third film, which should have been *Barren Lives* but ended up being *Mandacaru Vermelho* [*Red Cactus*, 1961], the point of departure was so-called private money. There was no support. There was no government agency. A large part of the money was invested by Danilo Trelles, a Uruguayan producer, who put some money into the film's production. I had the film stock from the German company DEFA, and in exchange I had to give it something filmed about Brazil in order to put together an international documentary about hunger. After that, all I had was each person's desire, each member of the crew. The adventure ended because it rained a lot and I didn't make *Barren Lives.* I ended up making *Mandacaru Vermelho,* a completely improvised film.

The next experience was *Gold Mouth* [*Boca de Ouro,* 1963], which was a production by Herbert Richers, a producer and distributor from Rio who is very well established. Herbert decided to produce this film and invited me to direct. I made *Gold Mouth* as a contracted director, then right afterwards I went back to the *Barren Lives* project, on which Herbert worked as producer. Luiz Carlos Barreto and I borrowed money from the National Bank, a private bank which even today invests in film productions. So the National Bank financed two-thirds of the film and Herbert one-third. This was the economics of *Barren Lives.*

After *Barren Lives,* I made a film called *El Justicero.* [The Enforcer; 1967]. This movie was made with government money, which came from a tax on profits of companies that distribute foreign films in Brazil. Part of this tax was devoted to producing Brazilian films. If the distributors wanted to, they could invest in Brazilian films. I made *El Justicero* with an investment by Condor Filmes, a distributor of European films in Brazil. After *Justicero,* I made another film, *Hunger for Love,* also produced by Herbert Richers and Paulo Porto, an independent production without government money. After [*A Very Crazy Asylum* (*Azyllo Muito Louco,* 1971)], also an independent production, I used the tax money to make *How Tasty Was My Little Frenchman* with Condor Filmes. After *How Tasty Was My Little Frenchman,* I made a movie, coproduced with France, *Who Is Beta?* [*Quem é Beta?* 1973] that was produced privately by Gérard [Léclery] without French government money.

The Amulet of Ogum was the first film I made with money from Embrafilme. Embrafilme started a distributing company and began to make investments, that is, advances on the profits from the films. They financed 40 percent of this film. After *The Amulet of Ogum,* I made *Tent of Miracles* [*Tenda dos milagres,* 1977], totally with private money from Ronald Levinson, a banker, a man of finance who, in the end, produced the film like a patron of the arts. After *Tent of Miracles* I made *The Road of Life,* another film produced by private initiative, by a São Paulo company, Vidafilmes, which was also totally removed from Embrafilme. Embrafilme also distributed *Tent of Miracles* and *The Road of Life* because it was the only distributor of Brazilian movies that existed. Well, after *The Road of Life* I made a movie that was totally produced by Embrafilme—[*Memoirs*] *of Prison,* then *Jubiabá* [1987] also co-produced by Embrafilme, with the French Production Society [Société

Française de Production] and French television. Now there's *The Third Bank of the River,* a movie produced by French television. My whole career has alternated between independent production, government subsidy, joint production, all these different methods.

GO: I would now like to turn from the compositional and economic to the ideational and cultural environment in which your films were made. It seems to me that the attention given to political and philosophical ideas and the confrontation of various currents of contemporary thought by the Brazilian filmmakers of your generation were entirely different than those of our own directors, and thus an experience about which every detail would be helpful to audiences in the United States. To put it briefly, how was your own "mentality" constituted?

NPS: Let me begin once more by referring to the work of Joyce as a birthplace, in the sense that he writes about the family. What type of consciousness arises from families? The nuclear consciousness will later combine with other experiences, like baptism, daily life, psychology, and social history. This being the case, I'm going to first sum up what happened within a middle-class family, half of Italian descent, in the north of the state of São Paulo. I received a lot of Italian influence from my mother, who had a rather clear way of thinking in which religion didn't exist. In everyday life, there was no religious thought. Nor on my father's side. My father was a solitary man, from a very small family; he was an orphan and raised by the Masons. Because of this, my brothers and I always had great freedom of thought. There was no code on the level of thought, but there was a code on the level of behavior—let's say there was a pragmatic view of behavior; there was no religious explanation for behavior. The only standard of behavior you would follow was that which they themselves gave, in such a way that from my first contacts with literature in school and throughout high school, the political thought that could influence young people was always a free choice. I was open to receiving influences and to accepting them or not. My father's example is of a beautiful thinker. At that time during the thirties there was a lot of pressure from political parties, like the Fascist party, that was very successful in Brazil. A large part of the military adhered to fascist thought, of which racism was a part. My father was an enemy of the whole fascist tendency, of the whole movement.

Starting from that point, then, there were various trips on the train of history. The most important one was Marxism, especially after the war in '45. I was in school preparing for the university. Soon after the war, the Brazilian Communist party had enormous popularity. All the Brazilian intellectuals, even businessmen, were joining the Communist party. Young people as well. A student preparing to enter university had a totally favorable attitude toward the Communist party. It was very common for young people to be and to want to participate in the public activities of the Communist party. It was a bit of a trend.

In reality, Marxist thought wasn't very widely known in Brazil. Marxist literature was simplified. It was a translation from the Spanish, and even today the texts are very amusing, full of expressions from the Spanish language. This Marxist phase was, in reality, a second university for young people like myself, becoming aware of subjects that had escaped them, especially the economic question, the question of the country's economic history, of its whole development since the colony. In school, in junior high and high school, in the university, a more conservative view was taught; the subject of power relations between nations wasn't dealt with. One result for people who become familiar with Marxist thought is a historic view, in which the whole process of growth has its relation to history. This "quasi-university" function that the party had was used up by the time that the party's contradictions began to bloom. As history advanced, party organization became more closed. However, by 1956 we were already out of the party.

But the most important event that created the break between young intellectuals and the Communist party was the invention of so-called socialist realism. It wasn't accepted. It wasn't accepted because of the leadership exercised against this thought, this dogma, by Graciliano Ramos, the author of *Barren Lives* and [*Memoirs*] *of Prison*. He officially belonged to the Communist party, but intellectually he was very distant from that dogmatism, from that closed aspect. Graciliano was against it and it became known that he was an opponent of "socialist realism." I didn't know Graciliano. Young people in São Paulo also thought that it was unacceptable to impose those narrow ideas on artistic and literary creation. It was then that the movement in search of freedom began. You agreed with the programs to transform society, to defend the national interests, etc., etc., but on the cultural question there was great disagreement. And when the revolution in Hungary and the subsequent invasion by the Soviet Union took place, that was a moral event that made me leave the party. After 1956, I no longer participated in the activities connected with the Communist party, even though I had been labeled a Marxist. Graciliano was very important at this point because he made a trip to the Soviet Union and to other countries in the area, to the so-called socialist democracies, etc., and so on. He observed what existed, like in [*Memoirs*] *of Prison,* in which he tells how he faced the unknown, using the same methods of observation he uses in his work. Evidently, it wasn't a proper book, a propaganda book as the leadership of the party expected. This book was banned by the party. The party had a lot of influence over intellectuals, even to the point of giving a *nihil obstat* [official certification] to a writer's publication. [*Memoirs*] *of Prison,* which criticized the behavior of true and false revolutionaries with great humor, was banned and published posthumously.

When I finished *Rio, 100 Degrees,* I went to Paris with the film in 1956. In May of that year, there was an international meeting of filmmakers, where I presented the film, and then I was invited to the Karlav-Vary Film Festival in Czechoslovakia. At the time that I left Brazil, there was international publicity about the famous report on the Twentieth Communist Party Congress, which denounced the crimes of Stalin and the Soviet political system. Even though the report was published in two newspapers in Brazil, the Brazilian Communist party insisted that it was false, that it had been an invention of the bourgeois press. And the leadership of the party had so much power that the militants readily agreed that the report was false and all lies. In the middle of so many lies, I traveled to Europe, and when I arrived in France, the French Communist party itself was discussing that report and decided it was true.

When I arrived in Czechoslovakia, I encountered a climate of euphoria because of the fact that things were loosening up. There was already an anti-Soviet movement, an extensive anti-Soviet movement. A lot of kidding, a lot of jokes about the Communist party, among the filmmakers, playwrights, and particularly on the part of Jan Kadar, who was beginning to direct a film after years of being ostracized. When I returned to Brazil in August, I was interviewed by a magazine that had ties with the Communist party. When I began to tell stories about Kadar, about anti-Soviet feelings, about liberation, the journalist stopped the interview and accused me of being a traitor: "You are transmitting ideas of the enemy." I said, "This is the truth and I am a witness, like someone who returns from the war."

Soon afterwards, there was the invasion of Hungary. I noticed that that journalists and other militants were completely subject to manipulation by the party leadership. They really believed that that report was false. I also would have continued believing this if I hadn't made the trip. So at that moment, my Marxist phase ended. In reality, what happened for me was that these events opened up my thinking to other questions; it was the humanitarian aspect. Not humanitarian, but humanist. This humanist aspect of thought, which didn't come from Marxism but from some Marxists, especially in Brazil, who have the humanist tradition, was the positive side of the trip.

The other thing that I think had more influence on my development than Marxism was existentialism. Right after the war, this movement was discussed in the literary supplements. Sartre's theater was the best-known manifestation, the most publicized. Existential thought was very important because it gave me the key to my work, how to develop ideas in cinema. It gave me a tool for my work; it suggested a method of work to me. Sartre's theater was incredibly important in my education and to my generation. In 1949, I went to Europe on a scholarship I had won to study, but I really went to learn about cinema, about the French Cinémathèque. And there was a great debate between the French Marxists and the existentialists. I participated as a spectator in this debate. But my heart leaned more towards the existential side; I was sympathetic to it. I don't know why I feel that in my growing up, from my grandfather, from my parents, I had more focus on the individual, a view that always began with the individual, to which existential philosophy gave more room for action, together with its free, almost anarchist spirit, while the organization of the Communist party, its dogmatism, weighed heavily on my head, on my upbringing. I always had the tendency to free myself from all that, to throw it all out.

Another thing which I can't help but recognize also in my upbringing was the São Paulo School of Law. The São Paulo School of Law is a traditional school. One of the first in Brazil, but with a very pragmatic character. It's a true school of Brazilian society, where one becomes aware of how society is organized, how its legal and judicial system is structured, how it is manipulated, managed, handled, and molded in accordance with history. The atmosphere at the School of Law mirrored São Paulo society, Brazilian society. When I studied there, the school was really complex. For example, the department of economics was only just beginning. There was a department of political sociology that I also studied at, besides the law school. I didn't finish the program of human and social sciences, French sociology, and French anthropology. There was political sociology only at the American School. The School of Law, based on the experiences of Brazilian politics, of São Paulo politics, came out of the experience of the country's ruling elite. In reality, they were all political departments. This school has always had a great influence, and today's president of Brazil, Fernando Henrique Cardoso, was educated in the French school.

Another influence was a very superficial but very interesting reading of Freud's work. Because I have psychologist friends, I read Freud. The translation was in Spanish. There wasn't a Portuguese translation then. I don't know why one book stayed in my mind, it was *Jokes and Their Relation to the Unconscious* [1905]. I was very interested in that subject.

GO: Because of your relationship to that intellectual background, you have been widely perceived to be committed to the community, the group, and while that is not untrue, the expression of alienation has been a continuous thread throughout your work, and that seems worth asking you to comment upon.

NPS: These two themes are linked to the question of identity, of identification. When a [man] can't find an identity for himself, he becomes alienated. Or rather, he becomes alienated because he can't find an identity. When he finds an identity, he will find his roots, which he considers poor, ugly, fragile. The only solution that will allow one to avoid this sense of being inferior is to become alienated, to seek an identity elsewhere. In *Hunger for Love,* for example, this character is solitary.

In Guilherme Figueiredo's book, with which the film started, the female character says she's American, but she isn't. She's a rich Brazilian who becomes alienated and goes to live in the United States, leaving Brazil behind. There she becomes even more alienated because she starts to believe in an Indian guru. She's fleeing from a reality that she can't understand and becomes easy prey for an adventurer, who leads her to convince herself of many things; he leads her to unknown spaces of alienation, to the permanent revolution, which gives her two qualities: one scientific and the other Maoist. I was trying to place in critical perspective the existential despair that young people had experienced during the military dictatorship. In cinema, I dealt with the other point of alienation, the racial condition, as someone who would like to do a psychoanalysis of society would, by making it possible for the audience to reflect a little on their condition. Of course, I know that alienation is also connected to the general conditions of the country, of society. Alienation originates from a society that is unjust, unequal, where a lot of questions are avoided. These questions exist because in Brazil there is enormous social injustice, with little possibility of change, where a few families own all the land, where the laws are antiquated. A basic question is that of agrarian reform, which has been talked about since the last century; but up until now, nothing has been put into practice. A discussion about land ownership in Brazil is inevitable. And all these questions about voting rights were discussed before and after the military coup that happened in 1963–64.

Another thing that I find basic in Brazil is the rural issue, because when a just distribution of the land comes about, it will be possible to advance in the field of education. So, on this point, there should be a deep relationship between social questions and alienation because alienation wouldn't exist if these social problems didn't exist.

GO: Your linking of alienation to identity is critical for me, and I would now ask you to ponder the very complex question on the formation of your own identity, especially in relation to country, race, class, and gender—how some of these elements entered into your consciousness, were changed, discarded, and so forth.

NPS: Because of my education, my social situation, the social situation of my family, ever since I was little I had contact with all those whom people today call "the rejected," the poorest in Brazil, including black people. Due to my parents' independent attitude, the fact that they weren't prejudiced at all, I was never prevented from any friendships with other children, from having friends who were black and poor, or Japanese. I grew up having very open relationships. This was normal and how things were done inside my house. It was very different from that whitening of Brazil that shows the powerful, rich Brazilian, who separates himself from his reality and invents an imaginary reality, as if he were American or European. Official Brazil always wanted to show a Brazil that was educated, rich, and so on. In spite of my upbringing, I think that I also had this view. When I returned from Europe and from the trip in '49, our ship had to remain docked in Dakar, Senegal, and I was there traveling third class. I couldn't keep still because it was hot, so I went out to swim and there were a lot of people playing soccer. One day they decided to form a team of whites and another of blacks. Whites against blacks. There were a lot of immigrants on the ship: Italians, Germans, and naturally I was on the white side. So a black guy from Senegal, where Portuguese is spoken, shouted at me: "Brazilian guy, where are you going? Since when is a Brazilian white? You have to play on our side." Then I really realized that by comparing myself to the Germans, to the Italians, right? as if there were no difference, I really understood the meaning of being white. I think that I was a racist for the first time in my life when I discriminated against whites. I have a friend who worked with me on the film *The Amulet of Ogum,* and after the film he said, "Nelson, I cried during the film, because I was taught to look in the mirror and see white."

In the Brazilian case, this racial mixture creates a need for the existence of a character who is Brazilian. And this brings great difficulties—that of a racial identity. In reality, there shouldn't be the need for this identity, because of what really happened, which was a combination, a mixing of the races. I'm talking about identity on a very basic level, but I think that it is a serious problem. I don't know if in Brazil someday it will be possible once the social differences end, when all have the same standard of living, the same opportunities in society, I don't know if the racial question will be eliminated. I think that it is basic. . . . In reality, this question is hidden in Brazil; there is not much discussion about it. There isn't much attention given to this question. It's a little lost. Evidently today, there are groups of blacks who are leading the fight against discrimination; they have sown the seeds. There are plenty of studies about the subject. They will contribute to finding a solution, a way—but the situation is really serious, because it is hidden, and no one has the courage to face it.

This is a social problem; as I make many trips in the realm of ideas, I think I am still a being in the midst of navigating. It's very difficult for me to identify with such and such, but I have this way of thinking, this philosophical view of things. I think everything should be pretty open so as to find the way as long as there is a need for it. My identity is an identity in progress. Even though I'm sixty-six years old. It's so much in progress that I think I'm finding the freedom to be this way. Because for me, the need to find an identity means a process of imitating or creating an imaginary identity in myself. It's very, very much the desire to be someone close to perfection, isn't it? And this perfection is openly admitted, included in various lines of contemporary thought. The difficulty is really with patriarchal thought. So, I'm coming to the conclusion that I can act without having to worry about creating a character. Perhaps I even want to exist with a fragmented identity, from my upbringing, my education, all this influence that began at home. Basically I'm the product of an Italian family that came from the north of Italy to settle in the interior of São Paulo. I'm a São Paulo hick. At the same time there are other influences. A delightful little racial mixture, very rich, very complex, right? So it's very difficult for me to seek this identity, except through an idealized construction. I think that the whole process is one of accepting one's fragmented identity with complete freedom, with all its influences. I'm able to make films about popular religion, from African influences, from candomblé in Bahia. I still need to incorporate this religious thought into my world. My background is Catholic; I have a connection with that from my grandparents, from my mother. But in spite of the whole Catholic influence in Brazil, I'm not able to be Catholic. Being Catholic doesn't fit into my system of thought, although my way of behaving is close to Christian . . . but I don't need to be Catholic, to have a Catholic way of thinking, to reduce myself to Catholic thought.

GO: You have been concerned with the major problems of our century—racism, poverty, inequality, imperialism—and I would ask you to reflect on the process of your own engagement with these issues in your work over many years.

NPS: As I've said, race is a theme that, because of my upbringing, is incorporated into my existence. Ever since my first film, this issue has been very clear. That film [*Rio, 100 Degrees*] makes the position of black people clear, as well as the position of white people or those who consider themselves white, the nonblacks, and there is an identification between the black and the poor that is very characteristic of Brazilian society and also of other societies in Latin America.

There isn't much difference in the nuclear family of men, women, children, property, be it in the middle class or its reproduction on another scale in another society. There is a discrimination in relationships, because some people are black, discrimination because they are poor. This issue, as I've said, existed in my head before I began to make films. So by that time I already had two well-defined influences, one coming from Brazilian literature and the other from Brazilian painting. Jorge Amado was a very widely read author, and when I was young I greatly admired Jorge for his books and for the fact that he pulled back the curtain on a Brazil that was different from the Brazil I knew, which was restricted to the city of São Paulo. He opened up the landscape of Bahia to me, the customs of the people of Bahia, the religion. Another thing that Jorge Amado brought to attention, as did [John] Steinbeck and [William] Faulkner, was the man of the people, like the sailor, the laborer, the factory worker.

Another influence in my life, when I wanted to make films, was neorealism. The neorealists showed that it was possible to make movies in a country like Brazil, that it was possible to make movies with very simple equipment, without extensive resources. These two influences are very evident in my films. The racial question develops along with social class, a different social space, but another element comes in: religion, religious thought, the mystical world, which is part of man's reality but is not talked about very much because it's a religion that exists in everyday life, in the clothing people wear. I consider the racial question to be basic, very influential and important in Brazilian society. My eyes were opened to accepting democratization, the coexistence of everyone, and I think that in our society, this will happen someday. . . .

The other great issue, poverty, which is very linked to race, is a permanent theme in all my films; it's not possible to think about national identity without including the very serious problem of absolute poverty in some parts of Brazil. It's inadmissible for a man of the twentieth century to live alongside poverty, and the essential point in the struggle of anyone who wants to participate in the social movement in Brazil is the elimination of poverty. In Brazil there is a permanent struggle to reduce poverty. Obviously poverty in Brazil is a political question, because the Brazilian elites, "the lords of power," have to be aware of the threat of poverty because interests combine to make this situation permanent.

This isn't the first time this has been talked about. There have already been many authors and movements that have clearly condemned the suppression of this question. There are many effective measures to be taken in order to neutralize a political situation and the exploitation of labor, which has changed little since the time of slavery. Obviously, it depends on the region of the country; in São Paulo, for example, the social situation is more progressive. In Santa Catarina, in the south of Brazil, the relations between labor and capital are very modern, but going up towards the Northeast, the relations are very antiquated and very difficult. There is an archaic Brazil producing a quantity of people who have nowhere to live. The issue here is agrarian reform and it is the great message of the book *Barren Lives* and consequently of my film, which tell the story of that family with no property who sell their labor when the land is fertile. If it rains, there's work; if it doesn't rain, they go somewhere else and as migrant workers are dependent upon the land-owners. They live a nomadic existence until they get the idea of living in the city. In the city there is no longer the need to depend on the rain; in the city whether it rains or not they will be able to find a place to live and a school for the children. This book, written in 1938, anticipated the studies and surveys in economics and social sciences that weren't carried out until after the war. The author's vision has the quality of a close observation of reality.

So I'm always concerned, as in the case of [*A Very Crazy Asylum*], about the role of the poor in Brazilian society and of rich people's strong awareness that they have all the advantages because of the way the system is set up. The scientist [in that film] is like a priest: he has a lot of power, just as the clergyman is the lord of religion in that space. He proposes to help and thinks that [humans are] always suffering from mental illness, and that he will help to cure [them] with the Catholic, biblical principles of São Paulo. For the person who can't work, and who goes to the asylum and has shelter and food, this is the best moment [of] life. And so on. This disrupts the hegemonic view because there's no more professional class. And the landowners end up saying no, this type of treatment can't exist because it disrupts the economy and hurts our interests. The tone of the film is comic; it's not a realistic film about the total alienation of all the characters; but in the film, the relationship between the two societies, the poor and the rich, is clear.

The relationship between the rich and the poor is universal, the reason for this is called imperialism, and it exists within all international relations. In my film *How Tasty Was My Little Frenchman*, this is placed on a cultural level. In *Frenchman*, the Brazilian natives have great admiration for the French, more than for the Portuguese, yet the Indian leaders dream of being able to fight a war and conquer the Portuguese in order to avenge themselves of everything the Portuguese have done to their people. Obviously, the cultural process required them to gain power in their own culture; it's the only one they know and the only one they can follow. Yet it's a complicated and powerful cultural process. They have to prepare this prisoner that they're going to eat in order to receive his energy and strength. The prisoner has to develop himself as a great warrior; he has to show that he has courage, so he lives for nine months, nine moons, a period that gives the Portuguese an advantage.

These great issues of the century, and my concern with them, I think I inherited from the great Brazilian writers, especially because in Brazil there's a literature that's totally involved with these questions, in favor of those who suffer; what I mean is the question of racism and poverty. All of this is in Jorge Amado, Graciliano Ramos, and all the writers of the thirties who were dealing with the question of imperialism, the question of the relationship among cultures. And there's also my São Paulo origins, there is Oswald de Andrade and the whole cannibalistic vision that was established by him. Brazilian writers of this period were influenced by American literature, particularly Faulkner and Steinbeck. This universe of thinkers, writers who were worried about these issues, they were the universe that molded me. And cinema is also in it, a cinema that positions itself in favor of human beings, of individuals, of freedoms. Issues like racism were also fought and attacked in a very clear fashion, because cinema is art for the people par excellence. Many times I had problems criticizing the masses because the masses are heterogeneous. I was also molded by American movies. The first part of my formation was all American cinema, especially John Ford. The movies of my youth were very engaged with ethical issues. They were very Manicheistic. Good versus evil. All the structure on the side of good, values, religion, the family, and on the side of evil, chaos, destruction, selfishness—well, this was basically the influence of American movies. Also the way of filming . . . that classical form, with the very well defined frame, everything very clear with no distractions, and very clear-cut ideas. The whole second part of my formation was neorealism, at a time when I was interested in cinema as a form of expression because with American films, I was only a spectator. I would go to the movies and get involved in them. But during the second phase, I was already a member of the film club. I was becoming aware of the history of cinema—French realism, Russian cinema, etc. And then neorealism appeared in São Paulo right after the war. And then the time really came to make films. I felt totally ready to make films, to discuss this possibility. It was very clear that films could be made in Brazil, by virtue of neorealism's lesson—the lesson it taught us about making films, which Glauber Rocha later condensed into one phrase: "A camera in the hand and an idea in the head." Neorealism had more influence because of this than because of its themes; we weren't really connected to [Cesare] Zavattini and [Roberto] Rossellini because of their themes. I once said that the social situation in Brazil in relation to that in Italy is the following: Brazil lives in a permanent postwar situation. Neorealism concerned itself with social issues, but the explanation for those social disturbances was that they weren't issues essential to society. Those problems with the family, abandoned children—all this was because of the war. The war had generated those social issues, while in Brazil, without a war, without conflict, we live permanently in a very similar situation, one that gets more and more critical all the time and keeps growing. And in terms of abandoned children, the situation is so bad that what can one say? The family is also disturbed, mixed up, falling apart. And there is one continuing fact in our society, especially among the poor: hunger. Hunger is even more prevalent within our society. So it's basically this: neorealism was a lesson in production, not a thematic influence. On the contrary, neorealism was something that gave us the courage to go out and film—let's film in the street, you don't have to be a professional actor, you don't have to be a star, you don't need a studio, you don't need great equipment, you don't need big financial resources or a fortune to make a movie. As John Huston said, between the script and the completed film you go through the world of high finance, so in the case of neorealism this was the great lesson. In reality, Hollywood movies and Soviet films were made by the state, produced by the state. Neorealism was the only new form of film production that appeared in the world and that influenced all of independent production, the whole Third World, all countries that, like us, dreamed of making movies. The Nouvelle Vague also greatly influenced another generation, that of most of my Cinema Novo colleagues. When the Nouvelle Vague came to Brazil I was already on my way. The Nouvelle Vague and the American Underground created a school here in Brazil, a combination of the Underground and Nouvelle Vague.

There is [Joris] Ivens and also [John] Grierson, two great characters I knew and came in contact with. A short time ago, I wrote a study about Grierson in which I called him a comet. He really had something like a comet in him. He would pass by and leave a very visible trail, and he would leave something like this trail in the minds of many directors. He passed through Rio from Montevideo. The Ivens I knew, whom I met several times in Europe, was very different. He was an international filmmaker with great courage, present at all the great world conflicts. He was always leaning toward the left—the war in Spain, in China, Latin America, Chile—always present in these movements. But this aspect of militancy doesn't have much to do with me. Not as a filmmaker, no. . . . Grierson, in spite of being something very fleeting, quick, influenced me a lot. As a matter of fact, there's a book of his that was required reading at the time: *Film and Reality.* He made only one film, but he commanded many films and was political. He placed great emphasis on the filmmaker's need to be political. Cinema will not progress unless filmmakers have a good dose of politics.

An Interview with
Nelson Pereira dos Santos (2001)

DARLENE J. SADLIER: Can you talk about the history of your production company, Regina Filmes, and how it operates?

NELSON PEREIRA DOS SANTOS: Regina Filmes was created by Regina [Rosemburgo] Léclery in the beginning of the 1970s in order to make the film *Quem é Beta?* [Who Is Beta?; 1973], in which she played the lead role. Later on, I assumed control of the company along with my children. It's a family enterprise, almost exclusively focused on the production of my own films, with some exceptions. Ever since my first movie, *Rio, 40 graus* [Rio, 100 Degrees; 1956], I've produced my own films—a practice common to all directors who want to preserve the integrity of their projects.

DJS: What are some of the major challenges of being a filmmaker in Brazil today and how do those challenges compare to those of the past?

NPS: The challenges are many and varied. The main one continues to be that of making a good film—a challenge common to directors throughout the world. But I would like to comment on another challenge, which I consider to be basic in the process of putting together a film: How to find the material resources to make real that which may be considered merely a dream.

In the 1950s and 1960s, there was no government agency—apart from the censorship board—that was concerned with Brazilian cinema. Accordingly, the resources, money, and services had to come from the market itself, from the commercial distributors of Brazilian films that existed then, from the laboratories, and from the equipment-rental companies. At this time we began the practice of seeking bank loans, which, despite galloping inflation, were miraculously paid off by the fiscal due date.

Then the government began to participate in the production of movies. First the Instituto Nacional de Cinema (National Institute of Cinema) was created, then Embrafilme, a powerful state enterprise that patronized 100 percent of Brazilian film production. When Embrafilme shut down, Brazilian cinema suddenly became an orphan. That was when the system in place today was created, which is based on the laws of fiscal incentive. It's necessary to knock on the doors of companies, both private and public, to try to sell film projects to marketing executives.

We are currently experiencing the transition from indirect state support, by means of the laws of fiscal incentive, to direct government action, through an agency linked to the president of the republic. I hope without censorship.

DJS: Do you go to the movie theater? What kinds of films do you enjoy seeing?

NPS: I go to the movies, but not as often as I used to go ten years ago, when I tried to attend every film on its first day of exhibition. Today, well . . . I still like to see films in a movie theater, I try to keep informed of the commentaries of critics, friends, and colleagues, and I do everything possible not to miss any Brazilian films.

DJS: What special problems do you encounter with location shooting? How do you deal with them?

NPS: I've filmed the majority of my movies on location for economic reasons. When I began, it was very difficult—and expensive—to film in a studio. For example, how to film the exterior of a Rio *favela* [slum] except in the *favela* itself? The difficulty, which later became a pleasure, has to do with relating to the local community, almost incorporating oneself into it, and that demands considerable cultural and psychological openness by the entire film team.

DJS: Can you talk about your shift from making black-and-white to color films? How did this affect your filmmaking?

NPS: Just when I was almost learning to make black-and-white films, I was forced to begin filming in color, since this was what the market demanded. I'm dependent on the cinematographer; he is the one who has the last word. As a result of the technical conditions within our reach, we always work from the point of the existing or available color, on exteriors with the help of God, and on the interiors with the creativity of the set designers.

DJS: What do you mean when you say that you were "almost learning to make black-and-white films" when you were obliged to make movies in color? Were you trying to achieve something in particular with black-and-white films?

NPS: I was trying to be funny . . . I can say that I "learned" to make black-and-white films with *Vidas secas* [Barren Lives; 1963]—an innovative photographic experience with Luiz Carlos Barreto. I made two more black-and-white films with the cinematographers Hélio Silva and Dib Lutfi (*El justicero* [The Enforcer; 1967] and *Fome de amor* [Hunger for Love; 1967]) in which we intended to work on the photography like a painter works on a painting. When the Brazilian market definitively opted for color film (no exhibitor wanted to show black-and-white films), I was "obliged" to film in color and had to yield to the technical norms imposed by the laboratory.

DJS: You have worked with cameramen such as Hélio Silva and Dib Lutfi several times. How do you go about choosing your director of photography for specific films and how would you describe your working relationship with them?

NPS: Hélio Silva and I began together. We were assistants—he as cameraman and I as director—when we decided to organize an independent team to make *Rio, 40 graus*. We made a half dozen movies together. The same happened with Dib Lutfi, an excellent cameraman, who is famous for his magisterial use of the hand-held camera. I made *Vidas secas,* a radical experiment in black-and-white photography, with Luiz Carlos Barreto. I also have to mention the name of José Medeiros, an experienced director of photography who helped to make *Memórias do cárcere* [Memoirs of Prison; 1984] and *Jubiabá* [1987]. My working relationship with them was always based on establishing a partnership in making the movie.

DJS: You have worked as editor on a number of films. How do you work with your own editors?

NPS: The same can be said in relation to the editors with whom I have worked. A joint partnership with division of labor. I participate in the first cut and I leave the technical side of the final editing touches to the editor. I hold in partnership with him the right of the final cut.

DJS: On what basis have you selected certain works from other media (novels, stories, theater) that you have adapted for film? Do you tend to choose your own favorite writers, or is the choice determined by other factors? And who are your favorite writers?

NPS: The choice of a literary work—and I have adapted seven novels and one play—derives directly from the choice of theme that I wish to address. *Vidas secas,* for example, was selected because it was a book about the drought and its consequences—a theme that led to my writing of an original screenplay. After many attempts, I reached the conclusion that the book, which until that moment was "for consultation," was the film that I intended to write.

I'm naturally very fond of Brazilian authors, those that helped me to know myself and to know Brazil. They belong to different periods, are masters of styles that are also different, and, for inexplicable reasons, they have stayed in my head. Perhaps it has to do with a desire to pay back what they gave me by making their works better known through the media of cinema.

DJS: What is the role of music in your films? Do you think about the music when you write or shoot the film?

NPS: The music in the film is the last thing that I think about. It only enters when I'm finishing the editing. I fear that music will disturb or dominate the language of the film, which is sometimes very similar to a musical arrangement. I prefer to "listen" to the film first and then make use of music in ways that respect it as an artistic expression. I don't like music that is subordinate to the image or the editing; in that form it loses its importance and originality.

DJS: Do you approach filmmaking for TV differently than for the cinema?

NPS: Filmmaking for TV is like writing copy for a newspaper (I was a journalist for some years) while filming for the cinema is like writing a book.

DJS: What are some of your upcoming projects?

NPS: I always have many ideas in my head. As soon as I have the money in my pocket, I would like to make a film about the adventures of a slave in search of his freedom during the war with Paraguay. The title is *Guerra e liberdade* (War and Liberty). It won't be an epic film with battle scenes, troop movements, etc., but simply an attempt to reproduce that socially upward movement of the Afro-Brazilian, modeled after *Amuleto de Ogum* [The Amulet of Ogum; 1975].

DJS: Can you talk about working with nonprofessional actors? How do you choose individuals without acting experience for your films? Do you direct them differently?

NPS: I chose nonprofessional actors for my first films because there was an insufficient number of professionals to round out my cast. Given the strong racial prejudice then (in the 1950s), black actors were not used in movies (or the theater), with the exception of Grande Otelo. During this period, I launched many actors, blacks and others, some of them still acting today in the profession. Beginning with *Rio, 40 graus,* and continuing up to *Casa grande e senzala* [The Masters and the Slaves; 2000–2001] one will always find nonprofessional actors in the background of my films as the professional actors engage in dialogue.

DJS: What was it like working with Grande Otelo in the 1950s and later in the 1980s?

NPS: In *Rio, Zona Norte,* it began as a terrifying experience: working with Grande Otelo was a challenge for a novice director! But a friendship and respect were soon established that lasted until his death. Grande Otelo was always one of my guides, in my life and in my work.

DJS: Do actors look to you for directions on how to play a scene or do you rely upon actors to create their own rationales for what they do on the screen?

NPS: First of all, I count on them. I keep my heart and mind open for what they have and want to offer to the film. They are the masters of the piece. Later, they count on me to applaud them and celebrate the filming of each scene. They like it when I say at the end of the take: "It's in the can!"

DJS: In its May 2001 issue, *Cahiers du cinéma* posed several questions to a group of directors. I'd be interested in your responses to a few of the questions asked. What are some recent films that you have seen in movie theaters in Brazil?

NPS: *Abril despedaçado* (Behind the Sun), for example, by Walter Salles.

DJS: Do you know the percentage of national films to American films that are shown in movie theaters in Brazil? Can you comment on how this situation has changed over the last ten years?

NPS: I don't know the exact numbers, but I do know that there are many more American films being shown than Brazilian films.

DJS: What is the easiest way to see movies in Brazil?

NPS: The traditional movie theaters are being replaced by more comfortable and safe multiscreen complexes. But there is always the video store on the corner, where we can pick up those films not seen when they opened.

DJS: Has globalization affected filmmaking in Brazil?

NPS: That's still very difficult to analyze at this stage of the game. There are theoreticians who say that the principal effect of globalization is to provoke a cultural production more closely identified with our roots. I don't know.

DJS: In a recent [July 2001] interview in the *Gazeta mercantil,* you mentioned that *Fome de amor* was your favorite film because you were far freer with film language than ever before. Can you describe what this freedom entailed and if or how it translated into your later films?

NPS: I filmed *Fome de amor* with so much freedom that a script didn't even exist. Ah, yes! There was one condition: the cast was already contracted. But I never saw this condition as an imposition by the producer because all the cast members were my dearest friends: Leila Diniz, Irene Stêfania, Arduíno Colasanti. . . . I can say that I wrote the film with the camera. Even today, even with well-written scripts, I try to reawaken the same sense of total freedom in the making of my films.

DJS: The letter prologue in *Como era gostoso o meu francês* [How Tasty Was My Little Frenchmen; 1972] never fails to fascinate viewers. How did you arrive at the idea for this particular part of the movie?

NPS: Like a piece of journalism, the letter from [Durand de] Villegaignon to [John] Calvin summarizes the events surrounding the installation of the French colony in Rio de Janeiro, as well as the rigorous laws of the European Christian who is isolated in the New World in the midst of ludic and naked savages. The text of the letter was read by a famous speaker who was also the news announcer for a French newsreel that [has been] very well known in Rio since the Second World War.

DJS: *Estrada da vida* [The Road of Life; 1981] was enormously successful at the box office, but Brazilian critics seem to have been less enthusiastic than the public. Do you see a tendency toward a split between public and critical reaction to films in Brazil?

NPS: The Brazilian criticism at the time was influenced by cultural prejudices that included an aversion to this kind of music. But, yes, in Brazil there is this division between the critical and public reception of films about any subject matter.

DJS: *Cinema de lágrimas* [Cinema of Tears; 1995] is a retrospective about thirties, forties, and fifties melodramas, yet it is also a film about Cinema Novo as part of Latin America's filmmaking past. Can you comment on the relationship between these two kinds of moviemaking in the film? Of all the Cinema Novo productions, why did you select Glauber Rocha's *Deus e o Diabo na terra do sol* (Black God, White Devil; 1963) for the final scene?

NPS: My intention with *Cinema de lágrimas* was to render an homage to Latin American cinema. Therefore, I chose the golden age of Mexican cinema in order to remind viewers that, in this period, Mexican cinema was not merely a circumscribed phenomenon in that country, but rather a phenomenon that was open to the whole of the continent—including Brazil. I tried to show [that] the memory of Latin America's Cinema Novo, venerated by young people in cinematheques, lives together and fully with the melodrama that preceded it in the history of Latin American cinema. The choice of *Deus e o Diabo* came about because I consider the film the most representative of Brazilian Cinema Novo.

DJS: Has your idea about a popular cinema changed since 1975, when your "Manifesto por um cinema popular" was published?

NPS: I need to confess something to you: that manifesto wasn't authored by me, nor was it of my doing. It was a piece produced by the Federação dos Cineclubes [do Rio de Janeiro; Federation of Cinema Clubs of Rio de Janeiro] at the time. In spite of the populist intention of the "manifesto," the film public at the time that it came out was a public made up of cinephiles.

DJS: When you say that the manifesto wasn't authored by you or of your doing, what I understand by this is that the organization and publication of the pamphlet was done by the cine clubs. But the content still reflects your ideas at the time about the importance of Brazilian popular culture and the possibilities of a cinema based on this culture. Correct? I see *Estrada da vida* as a good example of this "new" kind of cinema that focuses on aspects of popular culture that have been ignored or even disdained by the privileged sector, and that was enormously successful with the public at the box office.

NPS: Yes, you are right. The content of said manifesto, if I recall well, is composed almost entirely of statements by me to the press.

Feature Films

Rio, 40 graus (Rio, 100 Degrees; 1956)
Brazil
Production: Nelson Pereira dos Santos, Mário Barros, Ciro Freire Cúri, Luís Jardim, Louis-Henri Guitton, Pedro Kosinski (Equipe Moacyr Fenelon)
Distribution: Columbia Pictures of Brazil
Direction: Nelson Pereira dos Santos
Screenplay: Nelson Pereira dos Santos
Photography: Hélio Silva
Editing: Rafael Justo Valverde
Music: Zé Kéti, Taú Silva, Moacir Soares Pereira, José dos Santos, Amado Régis
Cast: Jece Valadão (Waldomiro), Glauce Rocha (the young maid), Roberto Batalin (the naval gunner), Ana Beatriz (Maria Helena), Arinda Serafim (Dona Elvira), Cláudia Moreno (Alice), Antônio Novaes (Alberto), Modesto de Souza, Zé Kéti, Aloísio Costa, Domingos Parón, Al Ghiu, Jackson de Souza, Jorge Brandão, Geovam Ribeiro, Carlos Moutinho, Sady Cabral, Mauro Mendonça, Carlos de Sousa, Renato Consorte, Walter Sequeira, Pedro Cavalcanti, Valdo César, Artur Vargas Júnior, Elza Viany, Edson Vitoriano, Nílton Apolinário, José Carlos Araújo, Haroldo de Oliveira, Portela Samba School, United Samba School of Cabuçu
Black and white
100 minutes

Rio, Zona Norte (Rio, Northern Zone; 1957)
Brazil
Production: Nelson Pereira dos Santos, Ciro Freire Cúri
Distribution: Lívio Bruni
Direction: Nelson Pereira dos Santos
Screenplay: Nelson Pereira dos Santos
Photography: Hélio Silva
Editing: Mario del Río, Nelson Pereira dos Santos

Music: Alexandre Gnatalli, Zé Kéti
Cast: Grande Otelo (Espírito da Luz Soares), Jece Valadão (Maurício), Malu
    (Adelaide), Paulo Goulart (Moacir), Washington Fernandes (Figueiredo),
    Artur Vargas Júnior (Honório), Zé Kéti (Alaor Costa), Haroldo de Oliveira
    (Norival), Laurita Santos (nurse), Maria Petar, Ângela Maria (herself)
Black and white
90 minutes

Mandacaru Vermelho (Red Cactus; 1961)
Brazil
Production: Nelson Pereira dos Santos, Danilo Trelles
Direction: Nelson Pereira dos Santos
Screenplay: Nelson Pereira dos Santos
Photography: Hélio Silva
Editing: Nelo Melli
Music: Remo Usai
Cast: Nelson Pereira dos Santos (ranch hand), Sônia Pereira (niece), Jurema
    Penna (aunt), Enéas Miniz, Ivan de Souza, Miguel Torres, José Teles, Luís
    Paulino dos Santos, Mozart Cintra, Joã Duarte, Mira
Black and white
78 minutes

Boca de Ouro (Gold Mouth; 1963)
Brazil
Production: Jarbas Barbosa, Gilberto Perrone, Copacabana Filmes Ltda.
Associate Producers: Imbracine, Fama Filmes
Distribution: Herbert Richers Produções Cinematográficas
Direction: Nelson Pereira dos Santos
Screenplay: Nelson Pereira dos Santos, based on the play by Nelson Rodrigues
Photography: Amleto Daissé, José Rosa
Editing: Rafael Justo Valverde
Cast: Jece Valadão (Boca de Ouro), Odete Lara (Guigui), Ivan Cândido (report-
    er), Daniel Filho (Leleco), Maria Lúcia Monteiro (Celeste), Adriano Lisboa
    (Guigui's husband), Geórgia Quental (Maria Luíza), Maria Pompeu, Sulamith
    Yaari, Wilson Grey
Black and white
102 minutes

Vidas secas (Barren Lives; 1963)
Brazil
Production: Herbert Richers, Danilo Trelles, Luiz Carlos Barreto
Distribution: Sino Filmes

Direction: Nelson Pereira dos Santos
Screenplay: Nelson Pereira dos Santos, based on the novel by Graciliano Ramos
Photography: José Rosa, Luiz Carlos Barreto
Editing: Rafael Justo Valverde
Cast: Átila Iório (Fabiano), Maria Ribeiro (Sinhá Vitória), Orlando Macedo (the yellow soldier), Jofre Soares (landowner), Gilvan and Genivaldo (the boys), Baleia (the dog)
Black and white
105 minutes

El justicero (The Enforcer; 1967)
Brazil
Production and distribution: Condor Filmes
Direction: Nelson Pereira dos Santos
Screenplay: Nelson Pereira dos Santos, based on the novella *As vidas de el justicero* by João Bethencourt
Photography: Hélio Silva
Editing: Nelo Melli
Music: Carlos Alberto Monteiro de Souza
Cast: Arduíno Colasanti (Jorge, "El Justicero"), Emmanuel Cavalcanti (Lenine), Márcia Rodrigues (Araci), Adriana Prieto (Ana Maria), Álvaro Aguiar, Rosita Thomaz Lopes, Selma Caronezzi, Emilson Fróes, Thelma Reston, Olga Danitch, Octavio Bezerra
Black and white
80 minutes

Fome de amor: Você nunca tomou banho de sol inteiramente nua? (Hunger for Love: Have You Never Sunbathed Completely Naked?; 1967)
Brazil
Production: Herbert Richers and Paulo Porto
Distribution: Herbert Richers
Direction: Nelson Pereira dos Santos
Screenplay: Nelson Pereira dos Santos and Luís Carlos Ripper, loosely based on the story "História para se ouvir de noite" by Guilherme de Figueiredo
Photography: Dib Lutfi
Editing: Rafael Justo Valverde
Music: Guilherme Magalhães Vaz
Cast: Leila Diniz (Ula), Arduíno Colasanti (Felipe), Irene Stefânia (Mariana), Paulo Porto (Alfredo), Manfredo Colasanti (the dog's psychiatrist), Lia Rossi, Olga Danitch, Neville de Almeida
Black and white
76 minutes

Azyllo muito louco (A Very Crazy Asylum; 1971)
Brazil
Production: Nelson Pereira dos Santos Produções Cinematográficas, L. C. Barreto Produções Cinematográficas, Produções Cinematográficas Roberto Farias
Distribution: Ipanema Filmes
Direction: Nelson Pereira dos Santos
Screenplay: Nelson Pereira dos Santos, loosely based on the novella *O alienista* by Machado de Assis
Photography: Dib Lutfi
Editing: Rafael Justo Valverde
Music: Guilherme Magalhães Vaz
Cast: Nildo Parente (Simão Bacamarte), Isabel Ribeiro (Dona Evarista), Arduíno Colasanti (Porfírio), Irene Stefânia (Luzinha), Manfredo Colasanti (justice of the peace), Nelson Dantas (sacristan), José Kleber (Crispim Soares), Ana Maria Magalhães (cousin), Gabriel Arcanjo (captain), Leila Diniz (Eudoxia)
Color
83 minutes

Como era gostoso o meu francês (How Tasty Was My Little Frenchman; 1972)
Brazil
Production: Nelson Pereira dos Santos, K. M. Eckstein, L. C. Barreto Produções Cinematográficas, César Thedim
Distribution: Condor Filmes
Direction: Nelson Pereira dos Santos
Screenplay: Nelson Pereira dos Santos
Tupi dialogue: Humberto Mauro
Photography: Dib Lutfi
Editing: Carlos Alberto Camuyrano
Music: José Rodrix
Cast: Arduíno Colasanti (Jean), Ana Maria Magalhães (Seboipep), Eduardo Imbassahy Filho (Cunhambebe), Manfredo Colsanti (French trader), José Kleber, Gabriel Arcanjo, Luiz Carlos Lacerda, Janira Santiago, Ana Maria Miranda, João Amaro Batista, José Soares, Maria de Sousa Lima
Color
83 minutes

Quem é Beta? (Pas de violence entre nous) (Who Is Beta? [No Violence among Us]; 1973)
Brazil and France
Production: Regina Filmes, Dhalia Film
Direction: Nelson Pereira dos Santos
Screenplay: Nelson Pereira dos Santos

Photography: Dib Lutfi
Editing: André Delage
Cast: Frédéric de Pasquale (Maurício), Sylvie Fennec (Beta), Regina Rosemburgo (Regina), Dominique Rhule (Gama), Noelle Adam, Nildo Parente, Isabel Ribeiro, Manfredo Colasanti, Arduíno Colasanti, Luiz Carlos Lacerda
Color
92 minutes

O amuleto de Ogum (The Amulet of Ogum; 1975)
Brazil
Production: Regina Filmes, Embrafilme
Distribution: Embrafilme
Direction: Nelson Pereira dos Santos
Screenplay: Nelson Pereira dos Santos, based on the story "O amuleto da morte" by Francisco Santos
Photography: Hélio Silva
Editing: Severino Dadá, Paulo Pessoa
Music: Jards Macalé
Cast: Ney Sant'Anna (older Gabriel), Anecy Rocha (Eneida), Jofre Soares (Severiano), Maria Ribeiro (Gabriel's mother), Emmanuel Cavalcanti (Mr. Baraúna), Jards Macalé (Firmino), Erley José Freitas (Pai Erley), Francisco Santos (Chico), Antônio Carneira, Washington Fernandes (Gogó), Ilya Flaherty, Luiz Carlos Lacerda, Waldyr Onofre, Antônio Carlos Pereira, Flávio Santiago, Russo, Olney São Paulo, Clóvis Scarpino (Clóvis)
Color
117 minutes

Tenda dos milagres (Tent of Miracles; 1977)
Brazil
Production: Regina Filmes, Ronald Levinson
Distribution: Embrafilme
Direction: Nelson Pereira dos Santos
Screenplay: Jorge Amado and Nelson Pereira dos Santos, based on the novel *Tenda dos milagres* by Jorge Amado
Photography: Hélio Silva
Editing: Raimundo Higino, Severino Dadá
Music: Gilberto Gil
Cast: Hugo Carvana (Fausto Pena), Sonia Dias (Ana Mercedes), Jards Macalé (young Pedro Arcanjo), Juarez Paraíso (older Pedro Arcanjo), Anecy Rocha (Dr. Edelweiss), Laurence R. Wilson (Dr. James D. Livingstone), Nildo Parente (Dr. Nilo Argolo), Jofre Soares (Colonel Gomes), Jorge Amorim (Tadeu Canhoto), Geraldo Freire (Gastão Simões), Severino Dadá (Dadá), Emmanuel Cavalcanti (Fernando Goés), Washington Fernandes (Pedrito

Gordo), Nilda Spenser (the contessa), Jurema Penna (Aunt Eufrásia), Fernando Amado (Lu), Arildo Deda (Professor Fontes), Geóva de Carvalho (Major Damião), Álvaro Guimarães (Astério), Gildásio Leite (Professor Fraga Neto), José Passos Neto (Prof. Silva Virajá), Manoel Bonfim (Lídio Corró), Maria Adélia (Dona Emília), Janete Ribeiro da Silva (Rosa de Oxalá), Ana Lúcia dos Santos Reis (Dorotéia), Liana Maria Graff (Kirsi), Luís da Muriçoca (Father Procópio), Guido Araújo (Prof. Calozano), special appearances by Menininha do Gantois and her "terreiro" following, Mirinha do Portão and her "terreiro" following, Mae Ruinhó de Bogum, the "terreiro" followers of Opô Afonjá, Mestre Pastinha, Caribé, Prof. Cid Teixeira, Jenner Augusto, Calazans Neto, Santi Scaldaferri, Mirabeau Sampaio
Color
142 minutes

Estrada da vida (Milionário e José Rico) (The Road of Life [Milionário and José Rico]; 1981)
Brazil
Production: Vidafilmes Produções Cinematográfias Ltda.
Distribution: Embrafilme
Direction: Nelson Pereira dos Santos
Screenplay: Francisco de Assis
Photography: Francisco Botelho
Editing: Carlos Alberto Camuyrano
Music: Dooby Ghizzi
Cast: Romeu J. Mattos (Milionário), José A. Santos (José Rico), Nádia Lippi (Madalena), Sílvia Leblon (Isabel), Raimundo Silva (Malaquias), José Raimundo (José Raimundo), Turíbio Ruiz (hotel manager), Marthus Mathias (Mr. Braulio), José Marinho (Joaquim), José Reynaldo Cezaretto, Nestor Lima, Manfredo Bahia
Color
104 minutes

Memórias do cárcere (Memoirs of Prison; 1984)
Brazil and France
Production: L. C. Barreto Produções Cinematográficas, Regina Filmes, Embrafilme
Distribution: Embrafilme
Direction: Nelson Pereira dos Santos
Screenplay: Nelson Pereira dos Santos, based on the book *Memórias do cárcere* by Graciliano Ramos
Photography: José Medeiros, Antônio Luiz Soares
Editing: Carlos Alberto Camuyrano

Cast: Carlos Vereza (Graciliano Ramos), Glória Pires (Heloísa), José Dumont (Mário Pinto), Tonico Pereira (Desidério), Lygia Diniz (Beatriz Bandeira), Ada Chaseliov (Olga Prestes), Waldyr Onofre (Cuban foreman), Arruda (Jackson de Souza), Wilson Grey (Gaúcho), Jofre Soares (Soares), Nildo Parente (union official), Ney Sant'Anna, Jorge Cherques, Marcus Vinícius, Fábio Barreto, Arduíno Colasanti, Tessy Callado, Stella Freitas, Ricardo Clementino, Antônio Amenjeiras, Jorge Coutinho, Procóprio Mariano, Paschoal Villaboim, Waldir Seviotti, Denny Perrier, David Quintans, Marcos Palmeira, Jurandir Oliveira, Erley José, Fernando de Sousa, José Kleber, Oswaldo Neiva, Mário Petraglia, Tião Ribas D'Avida, Rafael Ponzi, Cláudio Baltar, J. Barroso, Cachimbo, Herbert Junior, Cícero Santos, Chico Santos, Newton Couto, Sávio Rolim, Jayme Del Cueto, Rubens Abreu, Sandro Solviati, André Villon, Paulo Porto, Monique Lafont, Nelson Dantas, Fávio Sabag, Sílvio de Abreu
Color
197 minutes

Jubiabá (Jubiabá; 1987)
Brazil and France
Production: Regina Filmes, Embrafilme, Société Française de Production
Distribution: Embrafilme
Direction: Nelson Pereira dos Santos
Screenplay: Nelson Pereira dos Santos, based on the novel *Jubiabá* by Jorge Amado
Photography: José Medeiros
Editing: Yvon Lemière, Yves Charoy, Catherine Gabrielidis, Sylvie Lhermenier, Alain Fresnot
Music: Gilberto Gil, Batatinha, Jorge Amado, Armando Sá, Miguel Brito, Jairo Simões, Zezinha Baiana
Cast: Grande Otelo (Jubiabá), Antônio José Santana (young Baldo), Charles Baiano (older Baldo), Luís Santos de Santana (teenage Baldo), Tatiana Issa (young Lindinalva), Françoise Goussard (older Lindinalva), Romeu Evarista (Gordo), Betty Faria (Madam Zaída), Ruth de Souza (Aunt Luíza), Zezé Motta (Rosenda), Raymond Pellegrin (judge), Henri Raillard (Gustavo), Julien Giomar (Luigi), Jofre Soares (Mestre Manoel), Alexandre Marzo, Mário Gusmão, Lívia Machado, Carlos Alberto Santana, Manfredo Bahia, Wilson Manfredo Bahia, Wilson Mello, Elaine Ruas, Edney Santana, Yumara Rodrigues, Eliana Pittman, Oscar da Penha, Leonel Nunes, Jurema Penna, Márcia Sant'Anna
Color
107 minutes

A terceira margem do rio (The Third Bank of the River; 1994)
Brazil and France
Production: Regina Filmes
Distribution: Riofilme
Direction: Nelson Pereira dos Santos
Screenplay: Nelson Pereira dos Santos, based on the short stories "A terceira margem do rio," "A menina de lá," "Os irmãos Dagobé," "Sequência," "Fatalidade," from the collection *Primeiras estórias* by João Guimarães Rosa
Photography: Gilberto Azevedo, Fernando Duarte
Editing: Carlos Alberto Camuyrano, Luelane Correa
Music: Milton Nascimento
Cast: Ilya São Paulo (Liojorge), Sonjia Saurin (Alva), Maria Ribeiro (the mother), Bárbara Brandt (Nhinhninha), Jofre Soares (the hit man), Chico Diaz, Mariane Vicentine, Henrique Rovira, Waldyr Onofre, Gilson Moura, Mário Lute, Vanja Orico, Laura Lustosa
Color
90 minutes

Cinema de lágrimas (Cinema of Tears; 1995)
Brazil and England
Production: Meta Produções and the British Film Institute
Distribution: Riofilme
Direction: Nelson Pereira dos Santos
Screenplay: Nelson Pereira dos Santos, based on the book *Melodrama: O cinema de lágrimas da América Latina* by Sílvia Oroz
Photography: Walter Carvalho
Editing: Luelane Correa
Music: Paulo Jobim
Cast: Raul Cortez (Rodrigo), André Barros (the assistant), Cristiane Torloni, Patrick Tannus, Cosme Alves Netto, Sílvia Oroz
Color
93 minutes

Documentaries and Short Films

Juventude (Youth; 1950)
Brazil
Direction: Nelson Pereira dos Santos
Black and white
45 minutes

Soldados do fogo (Soldiers of Fire; 1958)
Brazil
Producer: Nelson Pereira dos Santos
Direction: Nelson Pereira dos Santos
Screenplay: Nelson Pereira dos Santos
Black and white

Um moço de 74 anos (A Seventy-Four-Year-Old Fellow; 1965)
Brazil
Production: Jornal do Brasil
Direction: Nelson Pereira dos Santos
Photography: Luiz Carlos Saldanha, Hans Bantel
Narration: Alberto Cury
Black and white

O Rio de Machado de Assis (1965)
Brazil
Production: Jornal do Brasil
Direction: Nelson Pereira dos Santos
Screenplay: Nelson Pereira dos Santos
Photography: Hélio Silva, Roberto Mirilli
Narration: Paulo Mendes Campo
Black and white
12 minutes

Cruzada ABC (ABC Crusade; 1966)
Brazil
Production: Alliance for Progress (USIS)
Direction: Nelson Pereira dos Santos
Black and white

Fala Brasília (Speak Brasília; 1966)
Brazil
Production: Ministry of Culture and National Institute of Educational Cinema
Direction: Nelson Pereira dos Santos
Photography: Dib Lutfi
Black and white
12 minutes

Alfabetização (Literacy; 1970)
Brazil
Direction: Nelson Pereira dos Santos

Cidade laboratório de Humboldt (Humboldt 73 City Laboratory; 1973)
Brazil
Production: Universidade Federal do Mato Grosso, Regina Filmes
Direction: Nelson Pereira dos Santos
Photography: Nelson Pereira dos Santos
Editing: Severino Dadá (assistant)
Narration: Samantha Lomba
Music: George André Tavares, Aloysio Aguiar, Villa-Lobos
Documentary about the Amazon rainforest

Nosso mundo (Repórteres de TV) (Our World [TV Reporters]; 1978)
Brazil
Production: Embrafilme
Direction: Nelson Pereira dos Santos
Screenplay: Nelly Moreira
Photography: Antônio Luís Soares
Cast: Nildo Parente, Helber Rangel, Waldyr Onofre, Washington Fernandes
Story about two boys lost in the Tijuca forest in Rio

Um ladrão (Insônia) (A Thief [Insomnia]; 1981)
Brazil
Direction: Nelson Pereira dos Santos
Screenplay: Nelson Pereira dos Santos, based on the story "Insônia" by Graciliano Ramos
Photography: Jorge Monclar
Cast: Ney Sant'Anna (the thief), Wilson Grey (Gaúcho, an older thief), Nádia Lippi (young woman)
Story about a young, inexperienced thief who robs a house and stays to eat in the kitchen while admiring a young woman sleeping nearby

A arte fantástica de Mário Gruber (The Fantastic Art of Mário Gruber; 1982)
Brazil
Direction: Nelson Pereira dos Santos

Missa do galo (Midnight Mass; 1982)
Brazil
Production: Regina Filmes
Co-production: Embrafilme
Direction: Nelson Pereira dos Santos
Screenplay: Nelson Pereira dos Santos, based on the short story "Missa do Galo" by Machado de Assis
Photography: Hélio Silva, Walter Carvalho
Editing: Carlos Alberto Camuyrano

Music: Glauco Velasques
Cast: Isabel Ribeiro (Conceição), Nildo Parente (the husband), Olney São Paulo (the youth), Elza Gomes
Color
35 minutes
Story about the supposed seduction of a young man by a married woman on Christmas Eve

La drôle de guerre (The Phony War; 1986)
France
Production: Bertrand van Effenterre, Edwin Baily
Direction: Nelson Pereira dos Santos
Screenplay: Nelson Pereira dos Santos, loosely based on a war diary by Raymond Queneau
Editing: Christian Billette, Henri Herre, Anna Bertona
Color
25 minutes

Casa grande e senzala (The Masters and the Slaves; four episodes, 2000–2001)
Brazil
Production: Channel GNT, Regina Filmes, Videofilmes, Maurício Andrade Ramos, Márcia Pereira dos Santos
Distribution: Riofilme
Direction: Nelson Pereira dos Santos
Screenplay: Edson Nery da Fonseca, Nelson Pereira dos Santos, based on *Casa grande e senzala* by Gilberto Freyre
Photography: José Guerra
Editing: Júlio Souto
Music: Villa-Lobos
Chapter 1: "O moderno Cabral"
Cast: Edson Nery da Fonseca (professor), Vânia Terra (student), Fernando de Mello Freyre Filho (Gilberto Freyre as a youth), David Carvalho de Oliveira (Gilberto Freyre as a child)
Color
57 minutes
Chapter 2: "A Cunhã, Mãe da Família Brasileira" (The Indian Woman, the Matriarch of the Brazilian Family)
Cast: Edson Nery da Fonseca (professor), Gheuza Sena (student), Antônio Candengue (director), Theater Company of Seraphim
Color
56 minutes
Chapter 3: "O Português, Colonizador dos Trópicos" (The Portuguese, Colonizer of the Tropics)

Cast: Edson Nery da Fonseca (professor), Ellyne Peixoto (student), Antônio Candengue (director), Theater Company of Seraphim
Color
55 minutes
Chapter 4: "O Escravo Negro na Vida Sexual e de Família do Brasileiro" (The Negro Slave in the Sexual and Family Life of the Brazilian)
Cast: Edson Nery da Fonseca (professor), Helena Menezes (student), Antônio Candengue (director), Theater Company of Seraphim
Color
58 minutes

Amancio, Tunico. *Nelson Pereira dos Santos: Catálogo (mostra de filmes e vídeos).* Rio de Janeiro: Centro Cultural Banco do Brasil, 1999.

Avellar, José Carlos. "The Backlands (Will It Fall into the Sea?). O'Grady, *Nelson* 36.

Azeredo, Ely. "O Novo Cinema brasileiro." *Filme e cultura* 7 (1966): 5–13.

Barbosa, Neusa. "Nelson Pereira dos Santos filma o clássico *Casa grande e senzala.*" *Cineweb* <http://www.cineweb.com.br/ent/ento501.htm>.

Beraba, Marcelo. "A Hora da Virada." "Manifesto," 3–5.

Berger, John. *Ways of Seeing.* London: Penguin Books, 1972.

Bernardet, Jean-Claude. "O amuleto mudou tudo." "Manifesto," 11–12.

Boucher, Philip P. *Cannibal Encounters: Europeans and Island Caribs, 1492–1763.* Baltimore: Johns Hopkins University Press, 1992.

Burch, Noel. *Theory of Film Practice.* New York: Praeger, 1973.

Canby, Vincent. "Barren Lives." O'Grady, *Nelson* 30.

Cárdenas, Federico de, and Max Tessier. "Entretien avec Nelson Pereira dos Santos." *Études cinematographiques* 93–96 (1972): 61–74.

Dessin, Joan. "The Tent of Miracles." O'Grady, *Nelson* 37–38.

Dyer, Richard. "Entertainment and Utopia." *Genre: The Musical.* Ed. Rick Altman. London: Routledge and Kegan Paul, 1981. 175–89.

Fabris, Mariarosaria. *Nelson Pereira dos Santos: Um olhar neo-realista?* São Paulo: Editora da Universidade de São Paulo, 1994.

Galvão, Maria Rita. "Vera Cruz: A Brazilian Hollywood." Johnson and Stam 270–80.

Gomes, Paulo Emílio Salles. *Cinema: Trajetória no subdesenvolvimento.* São Paulo: Editora Paz e Terra, 1980.

———. "Rascunhos e exercícios." *Crítica de cinema no suplemento literário.* Vol. 1. Rio de Janeiro: Editora Paz e Terra, 1982. 349–55.

Johnson, Randal. *Cinema Novo × 5: Masters of Contemporary Brazilian Film.* Austin: University of Texas Press, 1984.

———. *The Film Industry in Brazil: Culture and the State.* Pittsburgh: University of Pittsburgh Press, 1987.

———. "An Interview by Randal Johnson." O'Grady, *Nelson* 12–15.

———. "Toward a Popular Cinema." *Cinema and Social Change in Latin America: Conversations with Filmmakers.* Ed. Julianne Burton. Austin: University of Texas Press, 1988. 133–41.

———. "*Vidas Secas* and the Politics of Filmic Adaptation." *Ideologies and Literature* 3.15 (1981): 4–18.

Johnson, Randal, and Robert Stam, eds. *Brazilian Cinema.* Expanded ed. New York: Columbia University Press, 1995.

Jones, Patrice M. "Race Issues in Brazil Join Spectacle of Carnival." *Chicago Tribune* February 14, 2001: 1, 15.

King, John. *Magical Reels: A History of Cinema in Latin America.* London: Verso, 1990.

Lévi-Strauss, Claude. *Tristes tropiques.* 1955. London: Cape, 1973.

Lispector, Clarice. "De como evitar um homem nu." *A descoberta do mundo.* 3d ed. Rio de Janeiro: Livraria Francisco Alves, 1984. 412–13.

Machado, Rubens. "O cinema paulistano e os ciclos regionais sul-sudeste (1912–1933)." Fernão Ramos 97–127.

"Manifesto por um cinema popular." Rio de Janeiro: Edição da Federação dos Cineclubes do Rio de Janeiro, Cineclube Glauber Rocha, and Cineclube Macunaíma, 1975.

Margarido, Orlando. "A Imagem do Brasil." *Gazeta mercantil* July 20–22, 2001: 1–2.

Martín-Barbero, Jésus. "The Processes: From Nationalisms to Transnationals." *Media and Cultural Studies: Keyworks.* Ed. Meenakshi Gigi Durham and Douglas Kellner. Oxford: Blackwell, 2001. 351–81.

Mercador, Tonico. "Nelson Pereira dos Santos." *Revista Palavra* (Apr. 2000): 10–19.

O'Grady, Gerald. "Interview by Gerald O'Grady." O'Grady, *Nelson* 17–22.

———, ed. *Nelson Pereira dos Santos: Cinema Novo's "Spirit of Light."* New York and Cambridge, Mass.: Film Society of Lincoln Center and Harvard Film Archive, 1995.

Oroz, Sílvia. *Melodrama: Um cinema de lágrimas da América Latina.* 2d ed. rev. Rio de Janeiro: Funarte, 1999.

Page, Joseph A. *The Brazilians.* New York: Addison-Wesley, 1995.

Peña, Richard. "*How Tasty Was My Little Frenchman.*" Johnson and Stam 191–99.

Poppino, Rolli. *Brazil: The Land and the People.* New York: Oxford University Press, 1968.

Ramos, Fernão, ed. *História do cinema brasileiro.* São Paulo: Art Editora, 1987.

Ramos, Fernão, and Luiz Felipe Miranda, eds. *Enciclopédia do cine brasileiro.* São Paulo: Editora SENAC, 2000.

Ramos, Graciliano. *Vidas secas.* Rio de Janeiro: Livraria José Olympio Ed, 1938.

Ramos, José Mário Ortiz. "O cinema brasileiro contemporâneo (1970–1987)." Fernão Ramos 399–454.

Rocha, Glauber. "Uma estética da fome." *Revista civilização brasileira* July 3, 1965: 165–70.

———. *Revisão crítica do cinema brasileiro.* Rio de Janeiro: Editora Civilização Brasileira, [1963].

———. *Revolução do Cinema Novo.* Rio de Janeiro: Alhambra/Embrafilme, 1981.

Salem, Helena. *Nelson Pereira dos Santos: O sonho possível do cinema brasileiro.* Rio de Janeiro: Nova Fronteira, 1987.

Skidmore, Thomas E. *Politics in Brazil, 1930–1964: An Experiment in Democracy.* New York: Oxford University Press, 1967.

———. *The Politics of Military Rule in Brazil, 1964–85.* New York: Oxford University Press, 1988.

Staden, Hans. *Viagem ao Brasil.* Rio de Janeiro: Coleção Afrânio Peixoto, Academia Brasileira das Letras, 1988.

Stam, Robert. *Tropical Multiculturalism: A Comparative History of Race in Brazilian Cinema and Culture.* Durham: Duke University Press, 1997.

Tavares, Ricardo. "Land and Democracy: Reconsidering the Agrarian Question." *Brazil: The Persistence of Inequality* 27.6 (May–June 1995): 23–29.

Viany, Alex. "Cinema Novo: Origens, ambições, e perspectivas." *Revista civilização brasileira* 1 (Mar. 1965): 185–96.

———. *O processo do cinema novo.* Ed. José Carlos Avellar. Rio de Janeiro: Aeroplane Editora e Consultória, 1999.

Williams, Raymond. *Culture and Society.* Harmondsworth, England: Penguin, 1963.

Wollen, Peter. "Godard and the Counter Cinema: *Vent d'Est.*" *Film Theory and Criticism: Introductory Readings.* 5th ed. Ed. Leo Braudy and Marshall Cohen. New York: Oxford University Press, 1999. 499–507.

Xavier, Ismail. *Alegorias do subdesenvolvimento.* São Paulo: Editora Brasiliense, 1993.

———. "Golden Mouth: The Myth, the Media, the Domestic Scene, and the City in the Film by Nelson Pereira dos Santos." *Nelson Pereira dos Santos.* Ed. Gerald O'Grady. Los Angeles: Latino International Film Festival, 2002. 50–56.

Andrade, Mário de, 68, 71–72
Andrade, Oswald de, 67, 68, 71, 142
Angra dos Reis: as location for *Fome de amor,* 125
Animal Rights Association of France, 36
Anthropophagy, 64–65, 67–68, 71–73
Argentina: melodrama in, 114
Armendáriz, Pedro, 117
Armiño negro (Black Ermine) (film), 115, 118
Associação Brasíleira de Cronistas Cine-matográficos, 29
Astruc, Alexandre, 125
Atlântida productions, 6, 9, 29
"Atualidades francesas" (French Current Events) (film), 61
Awards/prizes, 2, 18, 33, 58, 86, 108–9, 130
Azeredo, Ely, 29–30, 33
Azyllo muito louco (A Very Crazy Asylum) (film), 50, 54–58, 78, 79, 131, 141

Bahia: influence on dos Santos, 140. *See also* Candomblé
Balança, mas nao cai (It Swings, but Does Not Fall) (radio program), 9
Baleia (dog), 33, 123. See also *Vidas secas*
"Baleia" (Whale) (Ramos), 35
Banco Nacional, 109
The Band Wagon (film), 94
Barbosa, Neusa, 1
Barcellos, Hugo, 28
Barravento (The Turning Wind) (film), 24
Barreto, Lima, 7
Barreto, Luiz Carlos, 33, 36, 102, 120n8, 128, 131, 147
Barros, André, 115
Beatriz, Ana, 13
Belle Epoque, 4
Belo Horizonte (film company), 4
Benário, Olga, 108
Bengell, Norma, 25
Ben-Hur (film), 25
Beraba, Marcelo, 86
Berger, John, 73
Bernardet, Jean-Claude, 48, 95, 121n17
Bethencourt, João, 49

Bicycle Thief (film), 8
Bienal exposition, 6, 9
Black-and-white films, 147. *See also specific titles*
Boca de Ouro (Gold Mouth) (film), 24, 25–28, 31, 79, 84, 131
Bopp, Raul, 68
Borges, Miguel, 24
Boucher, Philip P., 61
Boytler, Arcady, 117
Bracho, Julio, 117
Brakhage, Stan, 53
Brandt, Bárbara, 111
Brasílien (Staden), 58, 59, 60, 62, 63, 64, 65–66, 72, 73
Brazil: agrarian reform in, 141; class structure in, 78; dos Santos's alienation from, 79; easiest way of seeing movies in, 150; foreign interests in, 71, 72; French influence in, 63, 71, 74; intellectuals in, 53–54, 133–34; land ownership in, 136; national identity in, 70–72; 1935–37 coup in, 103; 1964 coup in, 103, 136; 1968 coup in, 53, 56, 58, 71; 1973 reign of terror in, 79; sex industry in, 89; U.S. influence in, 71; Vargas regime in, 101–9
Brazilian cinema: "Brazilian-ness" of, 7; challenges facing, 145–46; dos Santos's comments about, 89, 150; early national conferences on, 6, 10; in early 1960s, 28–29; emergence of, 7; future of, 2–3; and globalization, 150; Hollywood's influence on, 30; and politics, 144; social realities in, 7. *See also specific companies*
Brazilian Comedy Theater, 6, 7, 9, 29
Brazilian Communist party (Partido Comunista Brasilero): banning of, 5, 6; and dos Santos as student, 5–6; dos Santos joins, 5; dos Santos leaves, 10, 120n6, 134–35; dos Santos's films commissioned by, 8; and ideational and cultural environment, 133; and ideology of Cinema Novo, 31; intellectuals break with, 133–34; popularity of, 133; in post–World War II years, 5; and *Rio, 40 graus,* 10; and Twentieth Commu-

Darlene J. Sadlier is the author of several books, including *An Introduction to Fernando Pessoa: Modernism and the Paradoxes of Authorship* and *The Question of How: Women Writers and New Portuguese Literature.* She is a professor of Spanish and Portuguese and an adjunct professor of communication and culture at Indiana University.

Books in the series Contemporary Film Directors

Nelson Pereira dos Santos
  Darlene J. Sadlier

Abbas Kiarostami
  Mehrnaz Saeed-Vafa and Jonathan Rosenbaum

The University of Illinois Press
is a founding member of the
Association of American University Presses.

Composed in 10/13 New Caledonia
with Helvetica Neue Extended display
by Jim Proefrock
at the University of Illinois Press
Designed by Paula Newcomb
Manufactured by Cushing-Malloy, Inc.

University of Illinois Press
1325 South Oak Street
Champaign, IL 61820-6903
www.press.uillinois.edu